Big Fat
Gypsy Weddings

Big Fat Gypsy Weddings

By Jim Nally

HODDER &
STOUGHTON

First published in Great Britain in 2011 by Hodder & Stoughton
An Hachette UK company

1

A Firecracker Films Production
Copyright © 2011 Firecracker Films Limited
Licensed by Zodiak Rights Limited

Written by Jim Nally

Picture Acknowledgements
© Tyson Benson
© Firecracker Films Limited
© UNP Limited

A CIP catalogue record for this title is available from the British Library.

Hardback ISBN 978 1 444 72982 5
Trade Paperback ISBN 978 1 444 72983 2
eBook ISBN 978 1 444 72985 6

Typeset in Plantin Light by Hewer Text UK Ltd, Edinburgh

Printed and bound in Australia by Griffin Press

The paper this book is printed on is certified against the
Forest Stewardship Council® Standards. Griffin Press holds
FSC chain of custody certification SGS-COC-005088. FSC
promotes environmentally responsible, socially beneficial
and economically viable management of the world's forests.

Hodder & Stoughton Ltd
338 Euston Road
London NW1 3BH

www.hodder.co.uk

With grateful thanks to all the gypsies and travellers
who so generously let us into their world

Acknowledgements

This book was only possible thanks to Liam and Tina at Channel 4, to Thelma at Nico, to Paddy, to Fenella at Hodder & Stoughton and to Mark at Zodiak Rights but the biggest thanks go to the entire production team at Firecracker Films, especially Jes, Jenny, Jack, Jo, Vicky, Daniel, Ben, Morag, Ben, Julie, Lizzie, Osca, Sam, Moira, Guy and Sue. Thank you all so very much.

Author's note

Thanks Jes Wilkins, Sue Oriel and Mark Soldinger at Firecracker for the break. Thanks also to Jo Cantello and all at Hodder & Stoughton, especially my Editor Fenella Bates for the guidance.

Thanks to all the contributors to *Big Fat Gypsy Weddings* for the material.

Thanks to Ian Gallagher, Dennis Rice, Kathryn Johnson, Jeremy Hall, Andy Wells, Paul Crompton, Max Williams, Tom Ash and Captain Mann for the encouragement. And thanks to the Nallys - Jim, Bunny, Helen, Jacqui, Claire – and to Lee Ryan and Greg Woods for the enthusiasm.

And lastly, thanks to Alison Clements for helping, to James Nally for distracting and thanks to Bridget Kathleen McGrath for everything else.

Contents

Introduction

Welcome to the wonderful world of *Big Fat Gypsy Weddings*! Gypsies and travellers are amazing people, but they live secretive lives on the fringes of society. After centuries of persecution, they are understandably wary of outsiders and seldom allow them into their world. We were fortunate enough to be welcomed in, and by picking up this book, you too have accepted a gilt-edged invitation into one of the most lively and vibrant communities known to man.

You'll read about the courting rituals, extraordinary weddings and fascinating lives of some of the most colourful members of the gypsy and traveller communities. This book will give you a real insight into a little-understood world, one that's in genuine danger of disappearing.

Because of their secrecy and their transience, gypsies

and travellers seem mysterious and intriguing to outsiders. Some find their non-conformist, nomadic
existences romantic, but the dominant perception of
gypsies and travellers – and that frequently aired by politicians, residents' groups and the media – is that they are
dirty, criminal, violent, tax-avoiding and antisocial.

The headlines speak for themselves: gypsy families not
'playing fair' over planning regulations; the 'nuisance' to
settled society caused by 'illegal' roadside encampments; the
environmental destruction from fly-tipping and the rubbish
left by gypsies after they leave a site; house-calling scams;
dodgy driveways; benefit fraud; too many children. The list
of accusations is almost endless. The impression left is of a
'shameless' community in need of stringent legal sanction.

Gypsies and travellers have become settled society's
bogeymen, *our* bogeymen. It's easy to see them as dirty,
criminal, violent, tax-avoiding and antisocial because that's
what we are repeatedly told on TV and in newspapers.
Because we don't know who they really are.

Faced with such negative press, some gypsy and traveller
families felt the time had come to show settled society who
they really are. These people opened up their lives to us on
the TV series *Big Fat Gypsy Weddings* (*BFGW*). The partici-
pants don't claim to be representatives or spokespersons for
their communities or their cultures. They just want to
demonstrate that gypsies and travellers are largely decent,
clean, hard-working, honourable people who live by our
laws and their own strict moral codes. And who love to party.

The TV series discovered vibrant, enterprising and
traditional communities clinging to old-fashioned values in

the face of an intolerant and invasive modern world. Viewers flocked to catch a glimpse of these erstwhile secret communities and their amazing social lives. *Big Fat Gypsy Weddings* was a phenomenon. The big fat frocks, the flashy carriages and the wild wedding receptions will be for ever etched into our memories. Beyond the bling, *Big Fat Gypsy Weddings* uncovered some eye-popping cultural insights. For the first time, 'gorgers', or non-gypsies, learned about gypsy and traveller customs and taboos on subjects ranging from sex, marriage and education to violence, money and the role of women.

In the *Big Fat Gypsy Weddings* book, we delve deeper into the fascinating world of gypsies and travellers. You'll meet some unforgettable characters and hear all about their lives. *Big Fat Gypsy Weddings* is packed with brand-new stories and people, as well as fresh insights into all the characters you know and love from the show. This book takes you beyond the big fat weddings into the very heart of gypsy and traveller life, from the cradle to the grave, so brace yourself for even more incredible revelations about a secret world. Sit back and enjoy!

CHAPTER ONE

'We Traveller Girls Grow Up Fast'

'We have to clean up all of the time; then, like Cinderella, we can put on a big dress for one day and it's all about us. That's why we do it.'

Inside the Claygate Caravan Site, near Chessington, Surrey, you can hear the muffled hum of traffic 24/7. It is hemmed in between two thundering major roads – the A3 and the A309 Kingston bypass – yet it can't be seen from either. Like so many of Britain's 5,000 council-owned traveller sites, it is out of sight. Out of sight and out of the minds of the local settled community.

The councils of Britain seem to like it that way, for traveller sites are invariably situated away from public view. Fenced off, hidden, they are generally close to other facilities the authorities like to keep concealed: sewage plants, rubbish tips, water treatment works, flyovers, airports. The places where no one wants to live.

The site is small: sixteen pitches, all taken by Irish and English travellers. From the outside, the only thing you can see over the six-foot wooden perimeter fence is a scattering of roofs – caravan roofs, shed roofs, some pitched, some flat, all different heights and widths. The entrance is ornate – black metal gates, black railings and brick walls. It's snazzy, more *The Only Way Is Essex* than traveller. Inside, the seemingly random roofscape suddenly makes sense. Each pitch has two caravans and either one or two small sheds. The site is orderly, well maintained, almost quaint. There are tarmacked drive-ways, tended patches of grass and trees. Each pitch is fenced off; the caravans inside sit close together. By house-dweller standards, there can be little or no privacy. The focal point of each pitch is the 'shed' – the large, functional blockhouse that contains washing machines, toilets, baths and showers.

In between the caravans, or 'trailers', in traveller tongue, lean, brown kids – mostly topless despite the chill – mess around with bikes and boxing gloves, sticks and stones. A barking sheepdog can't decide which group to play with. A fat piebald pony chews grass, oblivious. Two broad men with thick heads of hair, their arms chestnut-brown against snow-white vests, march purposefully through the chaos, seeming not to see it or hear it. They share the same metronomic side-to-side gait. It's a tough man's walk.

Inside one white, six-berth Tabbert Vivaldi trailer, eighteen-year-old Irish traveller Lizzie Lee assesses the result of her hard work – two hours of scrubbing. It's the eve of her wedding and she's already cleaned her marital caravan. Her last act as a single woman: training for her role as housewife.

The trailer is about twenty feet long and eight feet wide. Inside, the first thing you notice is that it's blazing bright. The front and back ends are all window, covered in suburban net curtains. The second thing you clock is the cleanliness. In a mist of Pledge and Cif fumes, everything zings. It's a busy space, yet there is no clutter. Every surface is clear and clean. There's not a glass or a spoon or a remote control in sight. For a family to live in a space this small, military-style order is vital to harmony and sanity. It's traveller feng shui.

At one end is the living room; cushioned seating is secured against the back and side walls beneath the net curtains. Above the windows gleam wooden cupboard doors. In the centre of the trailer is the kitchen. On one side, a fixed dining table and seats for two; on the other, the kitchen sink and hob; above and below, more cupboard doors. At the far end of the trailer, a bed stretches almost wall to wall. Squeezed in on one side is a tiny shower cupboard. Like every other spare inch, the shower cupboard is used for storage. After all, the earthly possessions of an entire family somehow have to be packed away inside these compact trailers. There's no last-resort loft space. Besides, travellers and gypsies don't take showers or use the toilet in their trailers, even if they have the facilities: all sanitary functions are carried out in the privacy of the shed.

The Lee family currently lives in this and a second, similar-sized Bordeaux trailer. Lizzie and her younger sister Margaret, thirteen, share the Vivaldi. Mum, Dad and Lizzie's other siblings – Charlie, eleven, Ann Jane, nine, and Simey, three – sleep in the Bordeaux. Dad and Charlie go out to work most days, pressure-washing. Travelling men and boys tend to do the jobs people in the settled community would rather not perform themselves– window-cleaning, tarmacking, tree surgery, collecting scrap and pressure-washing, which is the power-hosing of concrete, tarmac, roofs and anything else you want cleared of dirt and parasites. Like a lot of traveller men, Lizzie's father has asked not to be identified. Many of his regular customers don't know he's a traveller. If they did, they wouldn't employ him, or so he believes.

Lizzie's mother doesn't want to be shown either: she's camera-shy. Nevertheless, she's happy for her kids to step up and so we film and try not to get in the way as Lizzie prepares for tomorrow's big day. The day after that, she and her new husband, scrap dealer Johnny, will pull away in the virginal Vivaldi to start a new life together at his family's site in Watford, on the other side of London. Johnny, too, asks not to be identified. He's worried that if settled people find out he's an English traveller, they won't sell him their scrap.

Lizzie is a textbook 'Colleen', the Rose of Tralee – what Hollywood casting agents think every Irish girl should look like. She's pretty with fiery sunset-red hair and sky-blue eyes, porcelain skin, dimpled cheeks, just enough freckles and a mouth that smiles easily and often.

Her manner and outlook seem much older than her eighteen years, something she readily acknowledges. 'We traveller girls grow up fast,' she says in singsong traveller brogue. Traveller girls do tend to look older than what they call 'country girls', or non-travellers. Some put this down to their almost religious devotion to the sunbed; traveller girls are happy with nothing less than a chestnut-brown glow. Others say traveller girls look older because they've been prepared for adult life from a young age – far younger than teenagers in the settled community.

Lizzie, like many of the girls featured on *Big Fat Gypsy Weddings*, sees herself as a modern-day Cinderella. Being the eldest daughter – and unmarried – she is tasked with keeping the family trailers spotless and taking care of the younger kids.

She describes her average day. 'You get up, get the children ready for school, give 'em breakfast and whatever, then kick 'em off, clean up, take care of Simey and by the time you've got that done, they'll be back from school and then you have to make their food and clean up after that. Put them to bed for, like, half seven, eight o'clock. Then you probably go off for a sunbed or have a bath and then go to bed. That's every single day.'

Lizzie's parents consider her responsible enough to take care of the kids and their trailers, but that doesn't mean that she can come and go as she pleases. Like many traveller girls, Lizzie lives on the end of a very short leash.

'If I wanna go to the shop, I've gotta go, "Mummy, is it

OK if I just go to the shop for a minute?" and then I have to go with someone else, be back at a certain time, where boys can just jump in the motor and go. There's no answering to anybody.'

From birth, most traveller girls are closely protected and sheltered by their parents. Once a girl gets married, the role of protector passes on to her husband. Lizzie is not planning to burn her bra anytime soon.

'When you're married, you have to answer to your husband the same way you answer to your mummy and daddy. You can't ask him to wash up; you've gotta get up and do it. You can't leave it there! Like you still have to ask him, is it OK if I go here and there? You still have to go with him, or with another woman. You can't just go off alone.'

Some Irish traveller girls, like Lizzie, happily accept day-to-day drudgery over education or a career. Lizzie has never attended secondary school. Many travellers leave formal education early. Most we spoke to never went to 'big school'. Parents say privately that they withdraw their children after primary school for three reasons: to stop them being influenced by country, or settled, teens, to spare them from sex education and to rescue them from bullying. Their boys and girls are instead taught the traveller world's facts of life. Boys must learn how to provide for their family. Girls must learn to cook, clean and take care of kids.

From their early teens, traveller boys go to work with their fathers, uncles or older brothers. They learn skills that are in demand, that can travel and, in most cases, require little investment. Many of the girls leave school at twelve to train for a life of domesticity, both before and after marriage.

'I think I was about eleven or twelve when I left school,' says Lizzie. 'I know that is hard for you to understand, but there really is no need for the teachers to keep going, "You need to go to school. You need to go to school," 'cos we ain't going to be doctors or lawyers or anything. Housewives, that's what we're going to be.

'I can read a little bit, if I take me time, but if I'm trying to read really quickly, I can't. I wouldn't say I'm bad, like not terrible. I'm OK. I can read, like, doctor appointments, important things. I think that's enough for travelling girls.'

Of course, many traveller girls disagree, and later in the book we will meet some young women who are determined to have a career of their own, and cash to splash.

Whether they're planning to work inside the home or out in the world, however, young travellers and gypsies often share the same romantic ambitions. For Lizzie and girls like her, one momentous milestone marks her progression to adulthood – her wedding day. From the day a traveller girl is born, the preparations begin for the biggest day of her life. Tomorrow, Lizzie will get to be a princess, a Cinderella, but for just one day, a day she's been thinking about for as long as she can remember.

'Now I'm getting nervous because I want it to be the most perfect day ever. The biggest day of my life it will be, me wedding day.'

At eighteen, Lizzie's a relatively old bride by traveller standards. The average bride in Britain is aged twenty-eight.

In the travelling community, she's seventeen. Many get engaged before they are sixteen.

Last month, Lizzie's little sister Susie got married, aged sixteen, having met her husband two years earlier. Susie confirms that marriage means trading one set of restrictions for another. She warns Lizzie, 'Being married, it's not sunshine and roses. If you wanna go to parties or weddings or nightclubs, you can't just get up and go, unless he is going with you. And then maybe sometimes they don't wanna go and you probably really wanna go but he don't, so you can't go.

'If I knew any other girls getting married at the age of sixteen, even if they were marrying Prince Charming, I would still recommend for them not to get married, because when you're sixteen, you're still only a little baby.'

With Susie flown and Lizzie on the runway, their younger sister Margaret is left behind at Lee HQ to pick up the scrubbing brush. Although thirteen, Margaret's braces and baby face make her look younger. Maybe her youthful appearance is also down to the fact she's yet to experience a sunbed baking, or maybe it's because she's still to succumb to the daily scrubbing routine. Now it is her turn to man the mop. She's been pulled from school to be home-tutored in a single subject: the role of traveller woman.

'I went for about a year and a half to secondary school,' Margaret explains. 'I came out of it because my sister got asked for. Like the boy came in and said, "Can I marry your daughter?" and, like, Daddy said, "Yeah." So that's why I'm starting to clean, and that's why I've left school. 'Cos, like, they're getting married and I have to do everything.'

In two days' time, Margaret will sweat and toil in the knowledge that her two older sisters – belle of the ball Lizzie and married woman Susie – have slashed their workload by getting wed.

'When I get married, I won't be doing all that I have to do at home. I won't be washing up and cleaning up after loads of people. That's what it's gonna be like for Lizzie now. They won't be cramped and on top of each other. It's going to be easy.

'Ann Jane is only nine, so she won't be doing anything – she's too young. She'll be out there playing all the time,' explains Margaret. 'I do feel a bit like Cinderella. For me to stay here all by myself and do all the cleaning is going to be really upsetting.'

Unlike her older sisters, Margaret resents her role as domestic dogsbody. She doesn't skirt around her chief complaint: that boys her age have it easy.

'Girls have got it harder than boys 'cos we have to sit at home, mind children and clean all the time! All they do is just go out there and jet-wash part of a driveway. We do more cleaning. We do more work than they do, yet we can't go anywhere or do anything. They get to do what they want.'

Margaret isn't just losing Lizzie; the family's shedding the much-scrubbed, much-loved Tabbert Vivaldi trailer. Margaret now has to join her mum, dad and three younger siblings in the Bordeaux. Traveller families make big sacrifices to pay for their daughters' weddings.

'Six of us sleeping in the one trailer!' moans Margaret. 'I think it is going to be hard. Really cramped 'cos it's a really small trailer.'

> 'Everyone is planning their wedding! Weddings are very important. It is like every girl's special day and they want it as big as they can, especially the wedding dresses.'

It's easy to see why married life might appeal to some teenage traveller and gypsy girls, especially those who see themselves as real-life Cinderellas and dream that some-day their prince will come and rescue them from the household chores and their parents' rules. To some, getting married means comparative freedom, a reduced workload and a day enacting their childhood fantasy. After all, doesn't every little girl dream of being a fairy-tale princess? Some lucky traveller girls get to live out this daydream for real, so long as they toe the line – cook, clean and abide by the rules – Daddy will stump up for the wedding of their dreams.

Many traveller and gypsy girls fantasise about their wedding day long before they're even allowed to have a boyfriend. Take fifteen-year-old English gypsy cousins Cheyenne and Montana Pidgley. Both look distinctly out of place on a Sunday afternoon in Staines, a well-named blot on West London's landscape. On first sight, it's hard to see the real Cheyenne (pronounced 'Shy-ann') behind the fake tan, heavy make-up, long dyed-blonde hair and peaked sailor hat, tipped jauntily over her right eye. On closer inspection, she's slim, pretty and poised, with delicate features. Her short sailor jacket, white low-cut top, black-and-white patterned shorts and white trainers attract the male attention she clearly craves. Montana, even browner, is dressed like a girl who's been playing in her mother's dressing-up box. A striking dark-eyed brunette, she's sporting a wine-coloured ensemble, with a short skirt and black suede knee-high boots. Although Cheyenne seems a little reserved – Posh Spice-esque – she is usually the first of the two cousins to speak. Her chalk-dry humour frequently breaks through her ice-cool exterior.

Both girls proudly proclaim that they dress to impress. They are quick to point out that their style – and that of English traveller girls in general – is understated and modest. At least compared to that of the Irish travelling girls.

'They wear really revealing clothes, like boob tubes and bikini tops and tiny shorts,' says Cheyenne. 'If I went out like that, my father would pull me back by the hair and make me change. We cover up much more.'

Although they flash less flesh than Irish lasses, Cheyenne and Montana are just as determined to snare a husband – and soon. Young travellers and gypsies don't just rely on weddings, christenings and funerals to meet potential partners; they go to fairs – Epsom, Stow-on-the-Wold, Appleby, Ballinasloe in Ireland – and each Sunday they congregate at certain well-known, easily accessible landmarks, such as the Bluewater Shopping Centre in Kent and the Trafford Centre in Manchester. And at a car park in Staines.

According to the girls, on a Sunday afternoon this car park is the place to be. Cheyenne and Montana join throngs of travellers here every week to chat, listen to music, dance and meet new people. The more boys you meet, the better chance you have of finding Mr Right.

'Everybody goes,' says Cheyenne. 'I think it happens in a car park so the boys can drive around in their Transits and play music with the door open so we can have a dance-off.'

A 'dance-off' is last traveller girl standing, sometimes literally. Montana explains, 'A dance-off is like when a group of girls dance and the boys watch and call the name of the girl that they like most. Whatever girl is left at the end is the winner. Sometimes it can go on for two hours.' Montana is a regular dance-off champion; Cheyenne prefers to watch.

The cousins insist that, at fifteen, they are too young to have boyfriends. Daddy says they must be sixteen, or a boy must have the bottle to ask him first – another unwritten traveller rule. Yet, according to the girls, their wedding days are not far away.

Cheyenne says, 'I want to marry at sixteen ... about sixteen or seventeen, when I am ready, but not any older than that.'

Montana plans to wait. 'I will be about seventeen or eighteen. I would like to go with a boy for two years and then get married, to get to know each other. Any older than that and you'd be like a granny walking down the aisle. You'd need a walking stick.'

So, with their wedding days looming – Cheyenne's giving herself about a year to make it happen – small wonder they think of little else. In short, the girls need to meet Mr Right, and soon.

Perhaps surprisingly, though, their marital fantasies aren't primarily concerned with Prince Charming whisking them away on a white steed, or in a white Transit for that matter. Their wedding daydreams focus almost exclusively on one thing – their wedding dress.

'Oh God, I have thought a lot about my wedding dress,' says Cheyenne. 'I would have a very big dress, because it only happens once so you have to make it what you can. You're like a princess so that day has got to be very special to you. Like a fantasy.'

Montana chips in, 'All the cameras are on me. I would like a Cinderella wedding. Everyone dreams of a Cinderella wedding.'

'I'd like to have a Snow White one myself,' says Cheyenne.

This doesn't mean she plans to hire seven very short pageboys for the day. In the world of teen traveller girls, fairy-tales are often shorthand for a particular style of wedding dress. Cheyenne goes on, 'My dress would have loads of diamonds at the top and would be all tight and then it would go right out from the waist down, very big.'

Although the fifteen-year-old cousins plan to get married at different ages, they still hope to have a joint wedding. 'Me and Montana are planning on having a double wedding. We have been planning it with each other every day. That's very normal with travellers.'

According to Montana, 'Everyone is planning their wedding! Weddings are very important. It is like every girl's special day and they want it as big as they can, especially the wedding dresses.'

The girls' motivations for getting married soon aren't simply romantic; they see it as escape.

'I'd like to marry just to get my own life and not live by my mum and dad's rules,' explains Cheyenne. 'It is very strict. There are several things that you can and can't do, but it is more what you can't do that is the problem. Obviously, your husband isn't going to let you do everything you want, and you have to go everywhere with him, but it is better than being at home, I would say. There is much more freedom than what you get living with your mum and dad at home. I can't wait. Married life? God, that would be like a dream.'

> 'I'd like to marry just to get my own life and not live by my mum and dad's rules.'

English, Scottish and Irish travellers proudly claim an entirely separate heritage and culture from each other and from that of Romany gypsies. However, like Romany gypsies, most English and Scottish travellers could walk into a shop, café or pub and go unnoticed. Irish travellers are different. They stand out because of their unmistakable accent: terse, throaty, rapid-fire and often unintelligible to settled society. It sounds broadly Irish, yet it can't be traced to any one county or region of Ireland. Second- and third-generation Irish travellers in Britain – many of whom have never set foot in Ireland – still speak this way, and they still consider themselves Irish travellers.

Irish travellers stand out in another way: many of the girls wear skimpy and outlandish clothes – shorts that couldn't be shorter, bikini tops that would scream 'red alert' to the parent of any settled teenage girl. For a wedding evening, many of the Irish traveller girls aim to wear as little as is decently possible. Arguably the most striking and unforgettable spectacles from *Big Fat Gypsy Weddings* are the evening discos. While men slake their thirst at the bar, women and girls throw shapes on the dance floor with all they've got. Dancing doesn't get dirtier than this. It is truly a sight to behold.

Some of the outfits would be considered outrageous if worn at a settled-society do. A snapshot of one wedding evening reveals a girl sporting a short black see-through lacy dress, black stockings with white lace trim and white suspenders. She is nine years old. A younger girl wears a black evening dress with noticeable chest padding. All are thrusting their hips in a way that a settled person may well find overtly sexual and disturbing.

Nearby, three girls in their early teens gyrate in X-rated outfits. One, aged about fifteen, wears a tiny pink skirt and a matching bikini top, pimped up with diamonds. A second wears super-tight white trousers and a miniscule white top. Another wears an out-rageously short white skirt. This is topped off with a white, diamond-studded bra. As a rule, the older the woman, the less flesh she flashes. One thirty-something wears a pink strapless flamenco-style dress, split to the hip. All are putting in a shift.

As the evening draws to a close, men and boys join the

fray. Most watch from the side – eyes agog and mouths open. A handful of them dance. Next to the carefree bump and grind of their dancing queens, the boys look self-conscious, uptight and awkward.

Watching discreetly from the wings is a gorger woman who knows Irish traveller women better than anyone outside the community and has attended countless traveller weddings. Dressmaker Thelma Madine is the artistic force behind the very biggest and fattest gypsy wedding dresses. To travellers, Thelma is Armani; Nico, her shop in Liverpool, is Harrods or Harvey Nics.

The store interior is a kaleidoscope of shocking pink, gold, silver, blood red and emerald green – many traveller brides like their bridesmaids to clash as luridly as possible with their virginal white. It's like walking into an enormous box of Quality Street. The senses baulk. Colours fight. Sewing machines clatter. The only thing more rapid than the Janome 6600p sewing machine is Thelma's machine-gun Scouse chatter. She is certainly a force to be reckoned with. With her slim figure, long, blonde hair and heavy make-up, she's one of those women whose age is impossible to gauge, and she certainly won't tell you! Thelma has become a passionate champion of traveller taste and tradition. She is a ferocious defender of their lifestyle and customs, as well as a fearless critic of some of the less palatable aspects of traveller life. Thelma is as sharp and cutting as a quilting needle, but also sincere and deeply knowledgeable.

Because Thelma and her team spend so much time with traveller girls and their mums, they now consider themselves experts in their culture. As Thelma puts it, 'When you are doing fittings, you have a lot of time to talk, so I just ask a lot of questions about the traditions and why they do certain things. All the questions that people want to know but nobody asks. I think I probably know everything about them now.'

Thelma and her team have made some of the 'shock and awe' bombshell evening outfits worn by young girls that caused outrage in the national press after *Big Fat Gypsy Weddings* aired. Thelma says this outrage is misplaced and totally missing the point.

'We've made dresses for four-year-olds and their mum wants little bra tops. I did find that very uncomfortable at first, because I just couldn't imagine a little four-year-old in a dress like that,' Thelma reveals. 'They said, "I want you to stuff her for me," and I said, "No, I'm not doing that!" but when you go to the wedding and you see all the other little girls, then you see why.

'If you went to a wedding in Liverpool and a girl was dressed like that, everybody would go, "That's disgusting, you know. It's paedophilic." But at a traveller wedding, they're all dressed like that; it's just accepted. None of the travelling community – who are the only ones at these weddings, by the way, apart from me – looks at each other and goes, "Oh, that's disgusting," because they're all dressed like that.

'It is just little girls dressing up and mothers dressing up living dolls. That's it! There isn't any crime in that at all. Maybe it is us that are the criminals for looking at it like that and thinking that way. Why is it disgusting?'

Thelma points out that these girls are partying in the

bosom of their families. 'I mean, they don't go to clubs; they don't go to pubs. The only functions that they go to are family weddings, so they are always protected. Their parents are always there. The aunties, sisters are all around that dance floor, all watching this girl. Nothing is going to happen. So it's not like a sexual thing. They just don't talk about sex; they don't talk to their children about sex. It's completely different to the way we see it.'

As for the suggestive dance moves, Thelma admits she was shocked at first. 'I thought it was very sexualised, what they were doing. It was like they were putting on a display, like birds do to attract a mate.' Then she realised that they're simply mimicking their idols. 'These girls want an outfit like Beyoncé, like Shakira, so they move like Beyoncé and Shakira. They all watch MTV and copy the moves. Younger sisters see the older ones and think, That's how you dance.

'So, with the Irish girls, you could be forgiven for thinking they are prostitutes, the way they dress,' Thelma concedes. 'They show a lot of flesh and dance very provocatively. Of course, the truth is their morals are higher than those of country girls. Traveller girls live by a very stringent set of morals.'

To get to the bottom of what Thelma's talking about, *Big Fat Gypsy Weddings* spoke to four Irish traveller girls from London. The eleven-strong McFadden family is settled in a house in Hillingdon, on the outskirts of West London. The old family caravan sits on jacks in the driveway. A couple of wagon wheels lean against the front wall: decorative nods to their nomadic roots.

Three of the four McFadden girls wear skimpy denim

shorts and tight, brightly coloured tops. All are chestnut brown and totally at ease with themselves. On their way to a tanning session, they walk and talk with confidence and certainty. Shrinking violets they ain't!

The eldest, Josie, sixteen, catches the eye. She has depthless blue eyes, thick brown hair and immaculate white teeth. Loud, proud and passionate, it's clear she's the boss. She's wearing a cropped top covered in multicoloured hearts. As we are to find out, Josie definitely wears her heart on her sleeve. In five weeks, she gets married to a nineteen-year-old English traveller, Swanley Smith.

Barbara, fourteen, is a Josie clone, but smaller. She talks less than her elder sister but, sharp and succinct, often says more. Berry, twelve, is Josie Mark III, smaller still. Cousin Shannon, fifteen, is the only non-identikit McFadden. She has crimson hair that catches the sun, though she's happier in the shadow of her chattier cousins.

Despite the perma-tanned flesh on show, Josie insists there is an Irish-traveller dress code – it's called Daddy. 'If my shorts are too short or my top too small, then Daddy tells me and I change.'

They might dress like hookers, but Irish traveller girls – and many of their English gypsy and traveller sisters – live like nuns. For traveller and gypsy girls, there is one sacrosanct law: they must be virgins on their wedding day.

As Josie puts it, 'Staying decent and pure till marriage, that is literally number one. That is right at the top. That is definitely the single most important thing in a traveller girl's life.'

Any suggestion or claim that they've engaged in

anything more than kissing a boyfriend causes a girl to be 'scandalised', her good name lost for ever. If a traveller girl loses her reputation, she loses everything. She's ostracised by her community and left to rot on the traveller shelf. Boys won't ask her out. She may never marry. Even if she denies the claims made against her. Even if the claims aren't proven. The McFaddens reveal that they shun any girl who is 'scandalised', even friends. They can't risk guilt by association.

Josie explains that a scandalised girl can never recover her good name. There is no happy ever after. 'If you're scandalised, you are dirty. Your life is ruined,' she says. 'Oh my God, you shame your family. If the rumour was basically true or not, you are scandalised anyway. It is very unlikely you would get married. If you did get married, it would be to a fool. What we call a "gorme". She would be getting married to a gorme because boys in this day and age marry a travelling girl that is clean and decent, not like a red rotten one.'

Traveller families are desperate for their unmarried daughters to avoid scandal or gossip, at any cost. The stakes couldn't be higher. Scandal can be toxic to all their hopes and dreams of marriage and kids. As a result, traveller girls have to follow the strict rules of socialising and courtship imposed on them by the community. All the girls we spoke to are forbidden from smoking or drinking. They can't go anywhere – day or night – on their own. They can't be alone in the company of a boy or boys. They are not allowed to date a boy until they're sixteen unless their dad gives special dispensation. They are never allowed to be alone with a boyfriend. When they're dating, another girl

– preferably a sister – must be present at all times. Even when a couple gets engaged, the girl must be always chaperoned.

For a traveller girl to leave herself isolated, particularly in male company, is dire folly. When it is a boy's word against hers, the boy is always believed. A girl's defence – that the boy is lying – will fall on deaf ears. So say the McFadden sisters, girls on the frontline of traveller dating.

'It is his word against yours and people will take his side. They always take the boy's side because boys are boys, aren't they?' says Barbara.

The girls reveal they would be scandalised just for being seen out alone late at night, irrespective of the actual circumstances.

'If that happens to you, basically run, don't let anyone see you,' says Shannon. 'Do a Spiderman through the town.'

It is for this reason that the McFadden girls are insepara-ble. Barbara explains that this is their Defence Strategy Number One against scandal. 'You can't go out on your own, because if any travelling girl went out to meet a boy on her own, he could say that this happened or that happened. Boys generally do it just to make themselves feel big and proud, to give themselves a good name. I am not saying that every boy does it, but that is how you get scandalised.

'So for the safety of it, you just take your sister or some-one with you, because anybody can spread rumours. But if you were with someone, they can't. You tell people to check with my sister or my cousin. It didn't happen.'

'You have got to keep your name clear,' says Josie. 'You have got to be clean and decent in everybody's eyes. You can't let a rumour go around saying that you did this and you did that.'

Even to go out as a group, the girls have to seek permission from their parents, tell them where they are going, ring at regular intervals and be home by a certain time. 'There are loads of rules,' sighs Barbara.

Most traveller girls can't go anywhere frequented by country boys, like pubs, nightclubs, restaurants or even school. Josie left formal education at eleven. In the absence of knowledge about country boys, myths and misconceptions spring up, fear and loathing. Country boys have become traveller girls' bogeymen. It is a mirror of settled society's negative attitude towards travellers and gypsies.

'I wouldn't go out with a country boy if my life depended on it. Travellers keep together. That's it,' says Shannon.

Barbara agrees. 'You'd be scandalised for even talking to a country boy.'

Although the McFadden girls don't want to admit it, many travellers consider country boys to be 'dirty' and of low morals. Of course, the demonisation of country boys suits the travelling community just fine. It's a genetic masterstroke; after all, intermarriage is crucial to safeguarding their community's future. Their young women shunning outsiders is critical to the master plan. That's a surefire way for them to protect their values and customs.

Traveller girls can only attend traveller events: family christenings, Communions, funerals, fairs and weddings. As a result, their choice of potential husbands is comparatively limited. When you attend a traveller function, everyone seems to be in some way related. Intermarriage means many wedded couples – particularly in the Irish traveller community – are distant cousins. Husband and wife have often known each other throughout childhood. Because they know each other's families, they know each other's values and worth – both morally and financially. The girl's dad – ultimately responsible for sanctioning the marriage – seems to like it this way. Better the devil you know . . .

What it means for single girls, though, is added pressure. Competition between them is fierce. To crank it up further, the girls are expected to marry young. Josie is getting hitched at seventeen, just. Shannon, now fifteen, wants to be married by seventeen. Barbara, fourteen, says she'll wed at age eighteen.

As Josie explains, 'In our eyes, if you don't get married by twenty-five, then you are scandalised for being old and not being married. There is a reason why you never got married. If she is twenty-four, twenty-five, twenty-six . . . people start thinking, 'what's going on? You are a wrong 'un.'

There is yet another unwritten courtship rule for the traveller girl to grapple with: she is not expected to have more than two boyfriends before she marries. Any more may be considered indecent.

So, from their early teens, the race is on for a traveller girl to hook the best possible catch from an ever-decreasing gene pool. Cue the eye-watering wedding evening outfits and Cinderella's soft-porn dance moves.

On the other hand, traveller boys don't seem to be burdened by any of these restrictions. According to the McFadden girls, boys can do what they like when they like.

'A boy can get up and go on about his business. He doesn't have to come back. He doesn't have to say where he has gone,' says Barbara. 'He can just say, "See you later. I'll be back later on." Go off and do what he likes. They can't be scandalised.'

This apparent double standard is something that the McFadden girls are happy to put up with. It's a man's world and they like it that way. As Josie says, 'Man is a man. I mean, come on. They can do whatever they want, can't they? In my world, I wouldn't want it any other way. I wouldn't change anything.

'I think it is best for a woman to be brought up the way we are. It is a cleaner way of life. A man has got more respect for his wife, I think, when he knows that she is a clean and decent girl, like; he can't throw this boyfriend or that boyfriend in your face.'

Barbara says that, ultimately, money talks. 'If you think about it, boys are the ones that go out working. Girls, once they get married, just tend to stay at home and want children. Obviously, it's the boys who put the money and the food on the table, so it is their world.'

> 'Boys are the ones that go out working. Girls, once they get married, just tend to stay at home and want children. Obviously, it's the boys who put the money and the food on the table, so it is their world.'

All of the *BFGW* girls agree that traveller boys are free to do as they like, but not all agree that this is how it should be. Noreen McDonagh, fifteen, from Queensferry, North Wales, is a smart, petite brunette with plans of her own and lots to say. Noreen has an open, expressive face and a magnetic personality to match.

She's something of a trailblazer in her Irish traveller community. She recently took her GCSEs and is waiting for her results. Now that she has left school, she is studying hairdressing part-time at college and also works part-time, at ABC Cakes in nearby Shotton. Noreen insists that she will continue to work after she marries. She's determined not to be financially dependent on her husband.

'My mother has always wanted me to work,' she says. 'She never, ever wanted me, as soon as I get married, sitting down in a trailer raising a load of children, no driving licence, no job, sitting down doing nothing, waiting for him to come back, cook, clean for him. Which obviously I would still do . . . but I would rather have a job so I'll always have me money there. If he does a runner on me, I'm not left with no money.'

When she applied for her job at ABC Cakes, Noreen made no secret of her traveller identity. What surprises her most is the collective shock of her traveller friends. First, that she landed a job. Second, that she is trusted by her bosses.

'When I got home from work first day, some of the girls is asking me, "But, Noreen, do you not find it awkward when you're working on the till? Do they look down at you to make sure you're not robbing any money?" I never once had that happen. They treat me with respect.'

Noreen has one foot firmly planted in settled society, which allows her to view her own community through our eyes. She doesn't like all that she sees. For a start, she doesn't understand why boys get such an easy ride. What irks her most is that traveller boys – unlike the girls – are fireproof to scandal.

'It's not fair. If a boy was going out with a girl and he was cheating on her, he's like, "I have got myself two birds there," and it's "Good on you!" Or if he was at a wedding and he grabbed five girls, "How do you do that, man?" Do you know what I mean? "Look at him, he's a stud. Look at him, he's getting all these girls." Honestly. Traveller boys just don't care. They will mess a girl about left, right and centre.

'But if I had a boyfriend and I was cheating on him with another boy, "Oh, keep away from that girl. Don't go around her. She's a bad girl. She is indecent." Anything can get rid of a traveller girl's name, just at the flick of a finger. The slightest little thing. That's why a traveller girl's life is so hard.'

According to Noreen, traveller girls can cope with keeping their homes and siblings clean – and their names cleaner still. What they can't handle is the very thing travellers hate most – virtual house arrest. More than anything, a strict and fussy dad will drive a traveller girl headlong into a shonky, make-do marriage.

'I reckon girls get married young because their mummies and daddies are too strict. They won't let them go nowhere; they won't let them wear shorts; they won't let them go off on a Sunday; they won't let them go off with boys. It's even got that bad that some mummies and daddies won't even let their daughter have a phone.

'Some girls think, Right, I'm going with this boy now – what? – three, four months. He'll do. And the boy realises how strict her life is and how much she wants to get out of her home life, so after just a few months, he'll go and ask to marry her. The girl will say yes just to get away.'

Noreen reveals another key reason for travelling girls marrying young – they want to look good in their wedding photos. She says, 'Most sixteen-year-old traveller girls look older than they are because of the sunbeds. It's the fake tan; it's their hair; they're just older in the face. And they think they're women at sixteen, and they want to get married young so that they look good in the photos. That's how important their wedding day is to them.'

While Noreen's studying, scrimping and saving go against traveller norms, when it comes to dreaming about her wedding, she's a traveller girl through and through. 'Every traveller girl wants to be a princess: the long hair, the sticking-out dresses, the big crowns. Some country people might find it tacky, but it's what we like and it's what makes us feel like a princess for one day. That's the best thing about it; that's the dream.

'When I get married, I'd like people to say, "Oh, the dress was lovely. The cake was nice," because it makes you look good. Next time you're seen in public, people will be saying, "Oh, did you go to her wedding? Her wedding was lovely." So you're known for your wedding day, you're known for your dress, so you're known for at least something you've done.'

Storybook weddings demand fairy-tale cakes. ABC Cakes is no conventional patisserie; it specialises in big fat cakes for big fat gypsy weddings. These can range from fifteen-tier diamond-studded towers to five-foot neon-lit Camelot castles. ABC cakes are anything but easy: water-falls, moats, bridges, Bibles, limousines, models of the bridesmaids . . . you name it and they'll replicate it for you in sponge. Noreen is the icing on ABC Cakes. She's the inside woman, privy to all the latest traveller crazes. Noreen knows what traveller girls dream of. She's ABC's barom-eter of traveller bling.

As her boss Gill explains, 'If we're ever worried that we're going over the top with something, we ask Noreen and she puts us right. If she's OK with it, we know it'll be fine with the bride-to-be.'

Noreen knows their influences: 'Cinderella, Snow White, Beauty and the Beast, the Princess and the Frog. Traveller girls get most ideas for their bridesmaids' dresses, their own dresses and their cakes from cartoons, the Disney Channel. That's where they get their ideas for these big dresses. You're like, "Oh my God, that really is lovely." Over the top? Yeah, big time, because that's what princesses are known for. After your wedding, it's back to reality. That's why you want to feel like a prin-cess for one day.'

> 'Cinderella, Snow White, Beauty and the Beast, the Princess and the Frog. Traveller girls get most ideas for their bridesmaids' dresses, their own dresses and their cakes from cartoons.'

The largest nomadic group in Britain – the Romany gypsies – arrived in the UK over 500 years ago. Since then, both Crown and government have attempted to disperse, control, assimilate and destroy them. Until 1783, a person could be executed just for being perceived to be of gypsy origin. Even the term 'gypsy' is borne out of misunderstanding. The earliest known records of Romany people describe them as 'Egyptians'. Their true origin only came to light in the twentieth century. Gypsies have no connection with Egypt whatsoever. Studies of Romany languages suggest that they originated in India, a discovery the Romany themselves readily subscribe to.

The second largest group, the Irish travellers, or Pavee, are thought to have originally been dispossessed by Oliver Cromwell's sacking of Ireland in the seventeenth century, or by the Great Famine, some two hundred years later. It's possible that neither may be the case, as other academics point to records of a distinct Irish nomadic group with its own language and customs dating back to the thirteenth century.

Their origins are impossible to pin down because travellers don't tend to write their own histories and they've rarely trusted anyone to record their oral history. Persecution has a way of making its victims suspicious of authority and hostile to outsiders. Irish travellers have even developed their own special secret language. Known as Shelta, it is a cryptolect – a language drawn from two parent languages, in this case Gaelic and English, then twisted and altered in a series of coded ways to keep outsiders clueless.

Since 1976, Romany gypsies and Irish travellers are

legally recognised ethnic minorities protected from discrimination under the Race Relations Act. They enjoy similar status across much of Europe, but not in the Republic of Ireland. As well as Romany and Irish travellers, there are English travellers, as we have seen already, plus English gypsies, Scottish and Welsh gypsies and travellers, New Age travellers and travelling show people.

Even those settled in homes – about half of all gypsies and travellers – retain their ethnic identity. Just because they no longer live on wheels doesn't mean they cease to be gypsies or travellers. Although legislation continues to stifle their nomadic way of life – they simply can't stop where they like any more or set up their own sites – their numbers are growing. In fact, in Europe, Romany gypsies are the fastest-growing ethnic minority. In the UK, estimates put the total gypsy and traveller population at between 120,000 and 300,000.

Violet Anne Stubley is a twenty-two-year-old Romany gypsy from the idyllic village of Stanton-under-Bardon in Leicestershire. Often in a vest and tracksuit bottoms, Violet Anne has the air of a professional athlete. She's slim and toned, head to toe. Her brown skin glows, her curly brown hair shines, and her teeth dazzle, like a *Good Health* cover girl's. Her personality also brings to mind a pro sports-woman. She's no-nonsense, blunt and something of a pessimist. She tends to view her bottle of hi-energy iso-tonic drink as being half empty, rather than half full.

She has an independent streak, no doubt encouraged by her mum, Joan, and dad, Bill. Both her parents were brought up in trailers in the traditional gypsy way.

However, when Violet Anne was small, Joan and Bill decided to give their four children a more settled upbringing and education. Bill put in the hard shifts that enabled him to build a fine four-bedroomed brick home near Markfield, six miles from Leicester.

Violet Anne loved school, staying on until fourteen. For the past five years, she has worked as a receptionist at a hotel near East Midlands Airport. This is one receptionist you wouldn't quibble with.

Violet explains how she's always worked. 'As soon as my national insurance number came through, I signed up with an agency. It's the only way I could get me own money. You get some travelling girls, gypsy girls, won't get out of bed all day, don't want nothing in life. That's not me. I am independent, very independent. I can get up and go when I like. I've got my own money. I've got my own car.'

Violet Anne is proud of her Romany heritage, but her employers don't know she's a gypsy. 'They don't know I'm a gypsy at work, because I know I'd be out that door quicker than I come in. I've never told them I'm gypsy, because when there's been gypsies on the premises, they always say, "They're gypsies. Don't let them in." I need the money, so I daren't tell them.'

> 'You get some travelling girls, gypsy girls, won't get out of bed all day, don't want nothing in life. That's not me. I am independent, very independent. I can get up and go when I like.'

Irish traveller Paddy Doherty, fifty-one, runs the thirty-one-pitch Duchy Road Traveller Site in Salford, near Manchester. His face is a Rosetta Stone of hard-knock traveller life: a creased, weathered forehead, a nose punched too often and the strong jaw of a man who keeps in shape. What's more, he has arched 'You taking the piss?' eyebrows and twinkling eyes that exude mischief, charm and devilment. For Paddy, vest is best. You'll almost always find him in a tight white singlet, all the better to set off those meaty, tattooed arms and that pumped-up barrel chest.

Paddy walks the walk of a man who believes his own hype. He's a hard man – so hard that he's not afraid to display his soft side. The dad of five is married to Roseanne, or 'woman', as he affectionately calls her. Blonde, gentle, kind-faced Roseanne is another unforgettable *BFGW* character, whose big heart and wicked wit won her legions of fans.

Paddy and Roseanne have one daughter, Margaret, now married with kids. Paddy offers us a typically forthright father's perspective on how to raise a girl in the traveller way. His first decision was to withdraw her from school. For him, no secondary education is worth putting her through sex education.

He says, 'Well, my girl, the minute she come thirteen, they have got to go to the big school. I don't believe in that, because they're taught sex, which is so unbelievable. They're the things that I don't go into. I'm a man fifty years of age and it's a shame even talking to you now about it. You know what I mean? We don't believe in that. We don't believe in putting our children to big school for that reason, and that's not just from Irish; that's English, Irish, Welsh, Scots. All gypsies.'

Another traveller dad – who doesn't want to be identified – puts it more bluntly. 'Gypsies don't believe in sex before marriage. Girls should be pulled out of school about ten or eleven, before they go to secondary school, because when they get in there, they start learning things that they shouldn't learn. It can corrupt them. I pulled mine out at ten.'

Paddy admits he and other travelling dads are strict with their daughters, and that this is why the girls marry young. 'A lot of them get married to get away,' he says. 'Looking back, you're just being overprotective. It's a funny world. With country people, they talk about marriage as getting tied down. With travellers, girls marry so that they can stop being tied down, by their mum and dad.'

Paddy went toe to toe, and gloveless, against some of the hardest, maddest travellers that ever lived, yet when it came to protecting his daughter from scandal, he felt utterly powerless. Graver still, he knew that the loss of her good name would mean the loss of his.

'It's very easy for a girl to lose her name. They scandalise young girls like *that* and it's a shame. There's a lot of young girls very, very clean and decent, respectable. There are a lot of dirty bleeders who've given them a very bad, rude name.

'Anyone who's been with a young girl and then talks about it and brags about it, he's worser and he's dirtier. As well as ruining her life, he's ruining their family's life, the girl and her parents. It causes terrible feuds between families. I let me daughter get married young and me worries gone away from me then. You're not frightened any more.'

Paddy still sounds relieved, all these years later. 'So when she gets married in the house of God, you know you are going to be blessed. Once you marry under God's eyes and you get a special blessing, till death do you part, it's the greatest gift in the world, ain't it? I believe so anyway.'

Cousins Bridget Ward and Elizabeth Doran.
Elizabeth is in pink, as Bridget's best woman

Top: Bridget and her bridesmaids
Bottom: Joan with her fairytale carriage and bridesmaids

Pat and Sam on their wedding day

Sam on her way to the church

Thelma Madine, gypsy and traveller dressmaker of choice

Thelma helping Mary with her dress

Thelma's little helpers

Thelma working on Mary Connors' wedding dress from the Royal Wedding special

Mary with her 20ft train

Thelma helping a girl with her mini-bride outfit

Johnny making a surprise entrance at his wedding by helicopter

Cindy and Johnny on their wedding thrones

Josie and her family anxiously wait for
the taxi to the wedding

Swanley and Josie Smith at the altar

Swanley and Josie celebrate their marriage with a kiss

CHAPTER TWO

'It's a Man's World'

*'I used to fight for money and that is how I made my
living. That is how I got the price of my things – my car
and my home – just fighting for money.'*

Is the living really so easy for traveller boys and young men?
What are they looking for out of life? More crucially for the
husband-hunting traveller girls in Chapter One, what are
they looking for in a wife? It took time, but finally two young
single Irish traveller men agreed to put us in the picture.

For commuters on the Manchester-to-Wigan railway
line, the Duchy Road Traveller Site is on the left-hand side.
Alert train travellers are the only people likely to get a
decent bird's-eye view of the cosy thirty-one-pitch traveller
nest, hemmed in as it is between the busy railway line and
quiet Duchy, the feeder road to Salford. Passing motorists
are just that. Maybe a few clock the small side road,

highlighted stylishly in two-tone black-and-white kerbs. There's a flimsy yellow-and-black crash barrier flattered by the name. Catching the eye are the letters 'P.D.', three feet high, painted white, right in the middle of the road. Beyond that, the sharp-eyed would see a quaint fan-shaped wooden fence screening the entire site, save for the roofs of a chalet, two sheds and, to the left, a small caravan.

The snazzy chalet belongs to our friend Paddy Doherty, site caretaker. Paddy doesn't just take care of the site; he takes care of its occupants. The ex-fighter is the undisputed Duchy Road rule-enforcer, peacekeeper and – in extreme cases – tenant-remover. The letters 'P.D.', writ large, Tour de France style, in the middle of the road, are his initials. Welcome to Paddy Doherty territory.

The chalet befits his status as site godfather. It's a cream bungalow – big, brash and brand spanking new. Hacienda-like, it brings to mind the countless wide-fronted bungalows that fleck the Irish countryside. Its four large, leaded PVC windows always glisten. The white PVC front door is always open: P.D. site-management philosophy.

Paddy's glamour chalet comes with the big shed. The humble caravan next door is home to his youngest son, sixteen-year-old Martin Tom, another 1950s throwback. Martin Tom wears his thick black hair slicked back. His face is clean-shaven and tanned. He's slim and toned, in vintage jeans and Doherty-issue snow-white vest. Martin Tom has boy-band good looks, though his face is more weathered than his years. He has his dad's dark, knowing eyes and his breezy, carefree confidence. In fact, he reminds the crew of *X Factor* winner Shane Ward, another Irish traveller.

Martin Tom's trailer is simplicity itself. About twelve feet by seven, the Sterckeman Starlett has a double bed, a dinette with a fixed table, a hob and a sink. The cupboard contains only porridge, the fridge only 'pop'. The TV and computer game consoles are the Starlett's focal point. Martin Tom can often be found here as he is now, elbow to elbow at the table, deep in game world, alongside cousin and traveller pal Davey McDonagh. Both boys stare dead-eyed at the screen. They are completely motionless save for their feverishly twitching thumbs.

Davey, also sixteen, has the look of an extra from *Happy Days* or *Grease*. He's got mousy, gelled-back hair, dark eyes and symmetrical features. Today, he's wearing a baby-blue vest, Levi's and Converse trainers. He too is handsome. Unlike most traveller boys his age, his face is soft and young – maybe a little chubby. It's like meeting a young Gary Barlow, except he's got the voice of a fifty-year-old rough sleeper. Most traveller boys tend to sound much older than they are, like they've got chalk in their craw. Maybe it's the dialect, the hacking vernacular. Or maybe it's the gruff score to an already tough life.

While they game, Martin Tom and Davey describe how the world looks through their sixteen-year-old eyes. Their opinions are personal – and they disagree often – but the boys say that their views on money, work, romance and marriage are typical of most young Irish traveller men they know. Both agree to be totally upfront – about everything, even the delicate matter of the opposite sex.

Martin Tom accepts that traveller girls tend to have a far tougher time than the boys. 'Travelling girls, they've got a very bad life,' he says. 'Not all of them. Some of them have got the greatest lives in the business, the spoilt ones. But most of the ones I know have it tough. When a travelling girl gets up, she's got to help her mum clean, look after kids, and then she might not be allowed off to, like, the pictures with everyone because her daddy won't let her. You can get some really strict ones, which is a bit stupid. There's no harm in letting her go to the pictures, as long as there's someone there looking after her.'

Martin Tom doesn't suffer such constraints on his social life. That's one of the reasons he moved out of his parents' blockbuster bungalow into this low-budget two-berth trailer.

'Living in my mum and dad's chalet, it's not as good, because you come back late or whatever, you have to creep in, try not to wake them up and, like, it's awkward. Here you have your own space and you can do what you want. It's better.

'It's not nice when your mummy and daddy hear you talking on the phone. It's not like something that you want them to hear, is it? It's not like I'm saying anything bad; it's just personal.'

In many ways, Martin Tom's new home is typical of any teenager's personal space – just a lot neater and cleaner. Spotless, in fact. Because, while Martin Tom may empathise with the skivvying Cinderellas of the traveller world, he's more than happy to let women cook for him and clean his trailer. When asked if he takes care of his home, he laughs in disbelief.

'No, no, no, I don't do the housework!' he says, shaking his head. 'No, no, me mummy does all that there, yeah, me sister, like, but no one else, man. Fetching for me, cooking and cleaning up, wiping the floor.'

Davey nods his head in approval.

Traveller boys are bred to earn money. Most, like Martin Tom, start working in their early teens.

'I'm seventeen in two month. I stopped school since I'm eleven,' he says. 'I never went to high school in me life. Most travellers only go to primary school, so you get to learn to read and write. Most travellers is dumb and can't read and write. Me, I'm not the best reader, but I can read, like, the basic things. I can read what I need to read basically.

'When I was like thirteen or fourteen, I was always going out with either my brother Davey or me brother Johnny and working with one of them. You go out, like, with your brothers until you pass your driving test and then you can go out yourself.'

Martin Tom plans to take his driving test as soon as he can. For a young traveller man, a driving licence is essential. A licence to roam is a licence to earn. To become self-sufficient. To become a man.

For now, 'We do anything, anything what brings in money,' he says, 'mostly, like, jet-washing, gathering and selling scrap, paving, tarmacking. Anything outdoors really. There's loads of things that people do out working. I work every weekday and sometimes Saturday, if I get up early enough. You've gotta have money. No money, no women,' he says.

Unlike the *BFGW* traveller girls their age, the boys can do what they like after work, but they share one burning passion with their female counterparts – the sunbed.

Martin Tom explains, 'Every young body takes a sunbed. We like to go on a sunbed if your skin's looking rough or you're very white and you need one.'

Davey chimes in, 'Boys normally like sunbeds when occasions are coming up like Appleby Fair or Christmastime or Easter. If you're white, you'll go on every day. Like, if a wedding's coming up, we go to a sunbed every day to get a colour.'

The rest of their evenings are spent in the Internet café, gaming or meeting up with girls. During the week, only country girls from the settled community are likely to be out. While traveller girls are discouraged from even talking to country boys, traveller boys can go out and meet who they like.

Dressmaker Thelma Madine lays bare the double standard. 'The traveller boys aren't judged to the same standard as the girls. It is a completely different thing,' she reveals. 'They're not frowned upon for having a country girlfriend before they get married, when they play around or whatever. If they have a country girl, that wouldn't matter as long as they don't marry one.'

When we ask Martin Tom if he'd marry a country girl, his answer is straightforward: 'No.'

His dad later elaborates, 'He wouldn't marry a country girl in a million trillion years. No way. I'm not racist, but I don't want my name to go out of the traveller culture.'

Perhaps tellingly, these 'in-betweeners' are in no great rush to wed.

Martin Tom says, 'Hopefully getting married about twenty-one, twenty, somewhere around that age. It's a good age. You've lived your life.'

Davey wants it sooner. 'I can see myself getting married about nineteen, twenty, because you've lived your life, you've gone on holidays with the boys and had a laugh with the boys. But at the end of the day, you can't choose when you're going to fall in love, can you? It could be tomorrow.'

Their outlook is in marked contrast to most of the *BFGW* girls, who've set themselves daunting 'marriage or bust' deadlines. The boys know that only fools rush in.

'I know boys who got married at sixteen,' says Davey. 'They think they are in love, but they are not, because when they get married, like, they are constantly arguing. Before I get married, I want to know the ins and outs of the girl.'

It is just as well that both boys say they'd only marry a traveller girl, because when they outline their 'terms of engagement' for a future wife, it's hard to see how any country girl could meet their unbending, hard-line criteria. First and foremost, according to the boys, a wife-to-be must come baggage-free.

Martin Tom: 'I wouldn't want to go out with a girl and every time I walk with her somewhere, some fella would say, "Oh, I went out with her. I went out with her," or what-ever shit they come out with. If she's not had a boyfriend, you can always say, "I was first to her. I was the first man there." No one can ever talk about her.'

So what number of ex-boyfriends is acceptable? Davey's quick-fire reply: 'None.'

Martin Tom's more of a thinker. 'Yeah, obviously, I would like none,' he says, 'but maybe one. At a touch, two. Maybe.'

Needless to say, the ex-factor doesn't apply to travelling boys. 'Boys are different,' explains Martin Tom. 'A boy can have as many girlfriends as he likes, loads of girlfriends. The girls might call him a player. Like some boys get with lots of girls and brag about it, but it slowly comes into a bad name and the girls think, I wouldn't go out with him because he's a player.'

Martin Tom is a player, but thanks no doubt to the influence of his mum and sister, he says he sticks to one golden rule: 'I think that you should only ask a girl out if you like her. Otherwise you are just making a fool of her. You wouldn't want anyone to make a fool of your daughter or your sister.'

The boys clearly have respect for women, but do they have the same level of respect for women as they have for men? Their wholehearted, unreserved joint answer is a big, loud 'No!'

Martin Tom tries to explain. 'With a man, with a boy, you can have, like, certain laughs, but you can't with a girl. Yeah, it's like two totally different people, boys and girls.'

If a woman commands less respect than a man, then how will this shape their marriages?

Says Davey, 'None of us is the boss, but obviously boys has, like, more say over the girls because obviously man of the house. Do you know what I mean? But no one is the boss, that's what I reckon.'

While Davey feels, to paraphrase George Orwell, that one traveller spouse is more equal than the other, Martin Tom is forthright. As far as he is concerned, his wife is his property.

Martin Tom: 'It is like your wife is yours. I haven't got a clue about marriage, but what I think is your wife is property to you. She's yours. Stamp your name on her forehead.'

The teenage boys talk with certainty about the role of the traveller wife. Their only dispute is how the future Mrs D and Mrs McD might be best encouraged to cook and clean.

Davey says, 'It's her home. She'd have to take pride in her home. She'd have to clean it. Can't just leave it to go to the dogs. For a girl, when you're married, you clean up. That's all it is; housewives clean up. The boy has to tell her, "Right, you, cook and clean. You have to do this. You have to do that there." That's what it is.'

Martin Tom doesn't like the idea of dictating the chores. 'You shouldn't treat a woman as a slave, though,' he says. 'Obviously, a man can't, like, wash a child and do the clean-up, but the way you are going on, it's like you're gonna be ordering her about, putting down rules.'

Davey counters, 'It's not a rule, but a girl knows that's her job, the same as a boy's got to earn a living.'

Martin Tom: 'But it's not really fair.'

Davey: 'It's not wrong either. You'd be devastated if your wife can't cook or didn't clean.'

Whatever the rights and wrongs of traditional traveller life, Martin Tom is sure of one thing. 'I'd want to come home from work to a clean trailer and a hot meal. It will never, ever change to where a man stays home and cleans up.'

The traveller husband's rules extend far beyond the four walls of the marital trailer or home. According to the boys, the married man decides when his wife can and can't go out, and what she can and can't wear.

'My wife can go out if I am with her,' explains Davey, 'or she can go out if it's all girls, like going to the pub for a meal or on a hen night or going to the pictures, but she can't go out by herself and not with other men, unless I go too.'

Martin Tom explains why a traveller wife can't be left on her own in a place frequented by country men from the settled community. 'You have seen the way that travelling women dress,' says Martin Tom. 'If we leave the wife, then some country man is going to come up to them and try it on with them. Come out with some foul language to your wife, then you are like, "Right, you are getting it now." I am far from a violent person – I really truly am – but I don't think any man would let another man talk dirty to their wife.'

To prevent this unfortunate clash of cultures and frequent bloodbaths, the boys have devised a strict dress code for their future wives.

Davey explains, 'Most traveller girls will wear very unbelievably short skirts or tops or whatever, but if what your wife is wearing is too flashy or short, then it is up to you as the husband to tell her she can't wear it. They can't do it. Do you know what I mean? You can't wear anything short. It must be past the knee.'

'Yeah, past the knee,' agrees Martin Tom, 'and no belly tops, no halternecks.'

According to the boys, when husband and ruler isn't busy dishing out the orders, he can do as he likes.

'You can go whenever you want and come back

whenever you want,' says Davey, 'whereas a girl can't go off for two or three weeks and come back when she feels like it. She can't do that. She has to wait at home day by day. A boy can go off for the weekend drinking with his friends. He can go on a holiday with other boys, whereas a girl obviously can't. I reckon it is right. Do you reckon it is right?'

Martin Tom: 'Yeah, why not? Like we said before, it is a man's world.'

In their 'man's world', there is one issue over which they are bitterly divided: violence against women. Martin Tom insists that hitting a woman is plain wrong, end of debate. Davey, however, thinks that in certain situations husbands *should* slap their wives.

Says Davey, 'When you first get married, the woman will try and take advantage of you and I think that's why a man should hit a woman.'

Martin Tom shakes his head in disbelief. 'What?'

Davey goes on, 'If a woman is, like, trying to make a show of you, yeah, and tries to make a laugh out of you, like calling me all names in front of all the boys? Then you hit her, to tell her to cut it out. Just a slap, like. Put her back in place.' Registering his friend's disgust, Davey tries to justify his stance. 'I wouldn't unless she really pushed it. Because girls can get, like, tormenting. I mean, it's a bad thing, but if it comes to it, I would do it. It should be done because girls do tend to step out of line. Just get them back in the line. I reckon, anyway.'

Martin Tom is visibly shocked and says so. 'A violent Davey! So you reckon – let's get this out, right? – you reckon when you first get married, you should go?' He starts hitting his hands. 'If you love her, all the world, you're not going to knock her about?'

Davey mishears his friend. 'Did I say knock her out? I said give her a smack to put her back in place.'

Martin Tom tries to reason with his pal. 'So when you get married, you're going to bust her up? So after five days, she's going to have a head like Mike Tyson? What about if you step out of line? Would you like your wife to hit you?'

Davey has it all worked out. 'Obviously, she can try. If I step out of line, she can go to hit me. Of course, I'm not going to let her hit me. She can hit me, obviously, but I'm not going to take it. I'll hit her back. You can't be a bitch, can you? Like and let her hit you.'

Davey, on the defensive, reminds Martin Tom that he'd apply only minimal violence. He says, 'Like, I don't mean to kill her, like punching her black and blue, but I mean just slap her. Or if you don't hit her, just do a runner for three or four days, for a week, like go partying for a week. Then you go back and you say, "Try to make a show of me again, I'll go for two weeks next time." There is two ways of dealing with this: doing a runner or hitting her.'

Martin Tom warns Davey that domestic violence often spirals into the grimmest kind of kitchen-sink catch-22.

'If she steps out of line again in another couple of weeks, it's just you start getting into a routine then where you just keep hitting her. Slowly but surely, before you know it, then you got to beat her and she's rolled up in the corner.'

Martin Tom will resort to nothing more forceful than a firm talking-to. 'You can just sit her down and say, "Look, listen . . . " and give her a warning or . . . give her a good talking-to. At worst, I'd send her home to her mother for a couple of weeks and then go back to her. I'd rather put her at her mum's for a couple of weeks before I'd ever put my hands on her.'

Davey's not budging. Mrs McD won't be spared the rod. 'It would take a lot for me to hit her, but she's my property; I own her. I wouldn't like to hit her – I really won't like to hit her at all – but if it comes to it, you have to do that, don't you?'

Davey insists that his view is shared by most traveller men he knows. 'That's what most boys would do, like just put her back in line. The man has more say than the girl does because, like I said, it's a man's world.'

It's not Martin Tom's world.

'I didn't know this side of you,' he says, getting to his feet. 'I'm going out.'

> 'It would take a lot for me to hit her, but she's my property; I own her. I wouldn't like to hit her – I really won't like to hit her at all – but if it comes to it, you have to do that, don't you?'

Traveller boys readily acknowledge that they enjoy far more freedom than girls. They say that they've earned this freedom. If they can go out to work, then they can go out to play.

Once he gets his driving licence, a traveller or gypsy boy has to find a way to make a living. The boys say their role as breadwinner brings real everyday pressures. He must learn to provide for himself, then for his wife and the seemingly mandatory large family. He may have to find work not just for himself but for brothers, uncles and nephews. Of course, most men in the settled community go to work, but they tend to have some qualifications. Many get stable jobs with set hours and wages, holidays and pension plans. What's more, racism isn't usually a potential obstacle to earning a living. So how do travellers and gypsies survive? How do some seemingly make fortunes? We'll examine this later, but for now we'll find out how a traveller or gypsy boy with no qualifications scrambles onto the career ladder.

Improvisation is the key. A traveller or gypsy must be able to turn his hand to several different types of work. He learns skills that are in demand, can travel, are needed all year round and that require minimum investment in equipment or transport.

Twenty-year-old English gypsy Pat Skye Lee is a tree surgeon who – like other gypsies he knows – could branch out into all manner of trades.

'We will have a go at anything really,' he says. 'You get gypsies doing UPVC, other ones like me doing trees, you get scrap men, jet-washing, paving, patching up concrete. We will have a go at anything really.

'Whatever we are doing, we tend to try and be self-employed as much as possible. I suppose it is being your own boss. Gypsies don't like having a boss, but I can't blame them for that. I couldn't really work for someone else. I couldn't go from doing what I do now to a proper job.'

Pat is wiry with dark brown eyes, fair hair and a lean,

sculpted jaw, emphasised by one of those pencil-thin beards that frames the face like chinstraps. It makes him look like a skinny Justin Timberlake, but with a gypsy haircut. That's what Pat himself calls it: his hair is shaved at the sides, thick on top, with a short fringe and a ponytail.

Pat lives with his family on the 16-pitch Earlestown Traveller Site, right next to the railway line in Newton-le-Willows, near St Helen's. In search of work, Pat comes face to face with racism every day.

'It is not very easy to find work when you are a gypsy,' he says. 'You get quite a few people saying, "Oh no, gypsies, I am not having them do work for me." But I suppose that is up to them. They might have had a bad experience in the past or they might have heard stories. It is quite annoying.'

Far more annoying to Pat are the ruthless opportunists who exploit a gypsy's lack of legal muscle. 'I have done jobs for people in the past, and when they find out I am a gypsy afterwards, then they wouldn't pay me. Or they will say that they aren't happy with things, which is wrong really. They shouldn't be allowed to get away with it. They know there's no point me calling the police. The police would take their side straight away.

'It makes me angry, to be honest with you, very angry, that people can get away with doing that. And it must go on all over the country. But you can't let it put a downer on your day. You've got to have a positive attitude. You have to keep telling yourself, I am going to get a job today and people aren't going to mind that I am a gypsy. But it is hard.'

Pat never denies he's a gypsy. He just doesn't mention it until he's asked. However, he knows gypsies and travellers who assume a false identity to earn a living. Some adopt a different accent, or hide tattoos and piercings, or have their gypsy haircut shaved off. Pat has heard men deny that they're gypsies when directly asked. He'd rather go hungry than degrade himself in this way.

'If people don't want to employ me, then that is their choice,' he says. 'I go and find someone that is happy enough to have me working for them as I am, without having to change. You will find the occasional person. Like the gentleman whose trees we are trimming today. He knows that I am a gypsy and he is OK with that. That is good. You don't have to hide anything from him. You don't have to be worried about him finding out and getting difficult with the payment. So it is good to find people like that, but you don't find them everywhere.'

Pat knows that featuring in *Big Fat Gypsy Weddings* might cost him work – and money – in the future, but like most of those who agreed to participate, he's determined to challenge the settled community's preconceptions about gypsies and travellers.

He says, 'I agreed to be on the series to show people watching at home that we don't just sit around all day not doing anything, or that we are up to no good. I want them to see that people like me go out there and earn our money the honest way. I don't depend on anyone but myself.

'Like, when they see these big weddings, they are going to be wondering, *Well, how did they pay for that?* Well, this is how we pay for it. We go out there and earn our money just like anyone else would in a proper job, and we pay taxes. So just to let them know that.'

'He can be the dog's bollocks. He can be dressed like 007, but you just know that he's a traveller.'

Paddy Doherty was born in England, but he's not English. He's hardly set foot in Ireland, yet he's Irish. He's so settled in his bungalow that his name is on the electoral roll, yet he calls himself a traveller. This may all seem illogical, but nobody could be more certain of their roots than site godfather Paddy.

'I've been in Ireland, all together, say, in my life, for about three weeks,' he concedes, 'and yet I have got a very strong Irish accent. Me mother was from Ireland; me father is from Ireland; I was born in England. I love United! Love football! All of my kids was born here in Manchester. We're all of us Irish travellers, though.

'I would never be looked at as an English traveller. That's impossible! It's like calling a horse a donkey! An English traveller's an English traveller. You can't make an Englishman into an Irishman! I am an Irish traveller. Honoured to be an Irish traveller.'

Paddy's voice is, by his own admission, rough. The hacking vernacular of an Irish traveller is a verbal ID card. Some try to hide it, but Paddy is passionate about defending his traveller identity, especially in a society that can be hostile.

'Don't call me pikey! A pikey's a pike. It's the dirtiest fish in the water. It eats rats, horses, dogs; anything dead it will eat. It's dirtier than a rat. It's the dirtiest fish in the water. I'll say, "Who the fuck are you calling a pikey? You dosser." It's insulting me and it's insulting my family and my parents, me grandparents.

'You don't understand how hard it is for us in this world. We don't get nothing given to us. Don't get me wrong, there are a couple of bad travellers, like there's bad Englishmen. You do get a couple of fucking divvies, but we're all not the one people.'

Some believe the term 'pikey' comes from the word 'turnpike', a favoured gypsy stopping point, or from an old English verb 'pike', which dates back to around 1520 and translates as 'to go away from' or 'to go on'. The pejorative Irish terms for travellers are based on hard fact. The terms 'tinker' and 'knacker' come from traditional ways they used to make money. 'Tinker' is from 'tinkering', or 'tin-smithing' – travellers used to fix pots, pans and tools. 'Knacker' is from the days when travellers would buy dead or dying animals, then sell them to the knacker's yard.

Of course, these traditions have died out. Times change. Those who adapt best to change thrive. This is an evolutionary imperative. Although on paper traveller and Romany populations are increasing, it seems it's getting harder and harder for families to maintain a traditional way of life. Is there a danger that the entire traveller culture – resistant as it is to change – may become extinct?

'We are losing our way of life,' Paddy says. 'Children today, you can bet your life they won't be travelling all around the land. They will be lucky if they travel four weeks in the year when they grow up because there will be nowhere for them to travel to. So we're losing our way of life, but travellers will never die out. Travellers will always be travellers! The majority will never be ashamed of what they are and where they come from. You got a lot of well-to-do travellers who still proudly say, "I'm a traveller," or, "I'm a gypsy." We won't let it die out.'

Paddy says the secret to their survival is their unbending adherence to another evolutionary imperative – travellers socialise. 'Travellers will go five hundred miles to meet traveller friends, to be at traveller weddings or christenings or funerals. Travellers will never leave each other. That bond is there. It's like I can always tell a traveller. He can be the dog's bollocks. He can be dressed like 007, but you just know that he's a traveller. Even if you don't know him, he'll give you a nod. A traveller is a traveller. We can't be absorbed into another culture because we *are* our own culture.'

It's a culture – Paddy readily admits – that can be steeped in violence. In his teens, Paddy turned to scrapping . . . not metal but flesh. He became a bareknuckle prize fighter. Sometimes thousands are wagered on these organised showdowns.

He explains, 'I used to fight for money and that is how I made my living. That is how I got the price of my things – my car and my home, just fighting for money. There was a lot of money to be earned out of fighting at that time. If you get your face busted up because you lose, then you have got a bad face and a hole in your pocket. But if you win, you have got a smile on your face even if it is all broken up.

'But thank God no one ever dies out of it. You get very

bad faces, more than bad faces. A fight can last five minutes to two hours. And no one's allowed to get any water, no drink whatsoever. Or you can't stop and wipe your face. You got to fight until you drop. Or until you give best. "Give best" means you give in.'

Paddy is not the type to give best. 'I'd sooner die than to give best to a man. I wouldn't be able to live with myself, look at me children, look at me wife. I'd never be able to sleep with my wife again if I gave best during a fight, knowing that I'd just been degraded. Don't get me wrong, there's nothing wrong with men giving best. You've got to be a good man to do that. But me? Never give in! Never give in! And I know people will say, "That's a mad bastard." I am what I am.'

Perhaps the person who suffers most is nowhere near the ring: his wife, Roseanne.

'When Paddy used to go fighting, I was just down on my knees praying every minute, "Bring him back safe and bring him back not wounded too much." Thank God he never came back too bad.'

Traveller women are not allowed to attend these fights. Paddy acknowledges it is very hard on the woman, far from the ring. 'Your wife is at home and you're fighting and our sons are fighting and she's worried to death because she's not actually allowed to come. You don't have your wife come see your jaw getting broken, your boys getting smashed, a part of your face getting bit off. But they are going through a harder fight at home than we're going through.'

As anyone in the fight game will tell you, knowing when

to quit is as important as knowing how to duck. Paddy retired aged forty.

'No matter who you are, everyone has got to pull the handbrake, haven't they? Tyson had to pull the handbrake. You are too old; the young racers are faster.'

For Paddy, fighting meant a pay packet and prestige. His reputation as a fair-but-hard fighter has led to a new role on the bareknuckle circuit: referee. Paddy enforces the rules of the fight – no weapons, no kicking, no gouging or hitting a man on the ground.

'Well, I'm known for being a fair man. I am just respected, which is a nice thing. Now whenever fights go on, they say, "Get us Paddy Doherty to show us fair play." It doesn't make a difference who they are and who they are not if you have fair play. If it were my brother against another man, I would give that fella just as much respect as I give my own brother. That is what fair play is about.'

That's not to say Paddy's stopped fighting. He's just stopped doing it for money. Now, the only prize is pride. Paddy is keen to tell us why travellers are quicker to fight than settled people. He explains that it's all to do with honour. A traveller man must defend his name. In the Irish traveller community, a man's name is all.

'Dohertys amongst travellers are known for having a fight,' says Paddy, 'but they are fair fighters. They are known for that. Everyone knows who the fighting breed is. Not bully breed, a good name for fighting but a good name for fair fighting.'

You don't need to be Don King to persuade Paddy to fight. If he feels you've dishonoured his name, he will fight you – irrespective of your weight, reputation or wallop.

'I won't care how strong he is. You ask me for a fight and you bait me for two minutes and I'm there. Even if you're going to knock me clean out! You're going to make my face like the Elephant Man . . . I'd still go out that door with you! And I know what I'm in for before I start. I wouldn't give best to no man. No man! The only man I bow down to is God!'

It might sound Old Testament, but Paddy insists that violent encounters play a crucial role in traveller culture. He says it is the best way to resolve disputes.

'Traveller fights never used to end up in a gang fight. Honest to God. Listen, I know hundreds and thousands of travellers, and you'd never hear of it. It was always sorted out. They get their best man, you get yours, and you arrange a fight. Best man wins. And then that is it. Squashed. That is the true traveller way. All sorted. Instead of your family getting involved and your cousins and your brothers. Then it gets out of proportion and then someone gets hurt out of it.'

Paddy says the other significant benefit to settling a dispute by means of an illegal, one-on-one grudge fight is that it precludes police and the law courts.

'Now, if someone hurt you, you just get the police. You bring them to court. Our way of life is to fight. Then it's finished. Win, lose or draw, we shake hands afterwards. So there's no one going to prison and there is no police involved. When you get the police involved, it's a very, very bad thing to do in traveller culture.'

Paddy's disappointed to report that these old-fashioned, bareknuckle honour fights are no longer the norm. 'The whole fighting breed is dying out. Everything is gangs now. It's got heavy. Guns and knives and people jumping people. You could be the best man in the world, but if you have got nothing behind you, you are no good because the crowd will beat you before you beat your opponent. Because then you have got to think of your family, your kids, and say it is not worth the hassle. You have got to back off.

'When you're young, fighting's a great thing. It's a rollercoaster. I have had hundreds of bare fights, badly broke up and everything, but I have never pulled a weapon on anyone. If a man beats me, he beats me. I beat him, I beat him.'

However, gang violence means nothing's ever clear-cut any more. 'As you get older, you find out it's no good; there is no winner out of it. You don't win. You think you've won, but you don't win. Sooner or later, someone is going to come along and do you.'

The rough, tough traveller world is ablaze with tales of feuds and fights and men vowing vengeance. Paddy's been in national newspapers frequently, linked to various on-going skirmishes. He's reluctant to go into detail for two reasons – imminent court action concerning members of his family and to spare Roseanne.

'I just don't talk about violence to me wife at all. I don't even ring her. If I get into trouble, I'll never bring it back home to her. If me sons get into trouble, still they are not allowed to tell their mother. Their mum can't take that. What she don't see and don't hear can't hurt her. You can see the way she is now: just talking about it and she falls apart.'

Despite the escalating gang violence and continuing racism, Paddy insists that being a traveller is the best life that there is. 'We've got a lot of barriers. Could you ever see a traveller as an MP? No! It's never gonna happen, is it? A traveller going to Oxford or Cambridge? He'll never get there. But we're free! We are properly free people! Even on the sites, we're free. A traveller's lifestyle is the greatest lifestyle in the world now. Big time. Big, big time.'

CHAPTER THREE

Pride and Prejudice

*'Most travelling people are very clean and they
get called "stinking gypsies". It is so wrong.
I don't know where they get it from.'*

At the start of *Big Fat Gypsy Weddings*, we pointed out how gypsies and travellers are frequently the subject of five sweeping generalisations: they are dirty, criminal, violent, tax-avoiding and antisocial. For many travellers, one of these five outrageous accusations cuts the deepest, especially with the Romany: 'Gypsies are dirty . . .'

Gypsies aren't just clean; hygiene is an intrinsic part of their entire belief system. Inner cleanliness for the Romany is next to godliness. Many Romany insist that, by their standards, gorgers are habitually unclean. The misunderstanding occurs because settled people and Romany have set views on hygiene that are totally at odds with each other. Welcome to episode one of *How Clean Is Your Trailer?*

Gypsies distinguish between something being dirty and something that is innately unclean or polluted. The word *chikli* (from *chik*, for 'dust' or 'soil') means dirty in a harmless way, but the word *mochadi* means impure or polluted. Romany gypsies make another distinction. This one is between the inside of the body and the outside. The inner body must be kept pure. The outer body, or skin – with its discarded scales, accumulated dirt, by-products of hair and waste – is merely a protective vessel for the all-important inner self. It doesn't matter if a gypsy is *chikli* – black with dirt from working all day – so long as the dirt isn't taken into the inner body. Dirt on the inside makes someone *mochadi* – intrinsically polluted.

It's all about the inside. Anything put in the mouth must be thoroughly clean. Attention is directed not only towards food but also vessels and cutlery that are placed between the lips, the entry to the inner body. Chipped or cracked crockery must be jettisoned.

The primary distinction is between washing objects for the inner body and the washing of the outer body. The pure inner body must not come into contact with the *chikli* outside. Food and eating utensils must never be washed in a bowl used for washing hands, the rest of the body or clothing. Ideally, the gypsy has a whole collection of bowls: one for washing food, another for washing crockery and cooking utensils, one for the main laundry, one for washing the body, one for washing the floor and trailer. Gypsies speak more commonly of two bowls, distinguishing the crockery from the personal 'body and laundry' washing bowl.

Using this system, nothing from the outer body can pollute the inner body. No knife or fork will be corrupted by dirt from the skin or clothes. It is fastidious. The tea towel used for drying crockery and cutlery must be washed in the washing-up bowl, not with the rest of the laundry. The personal washing and laundry bowls are potentially polluting and so are often placed outside the trailer. The crockery washing-up bowl takes pride of place inside.

Clothes-washing, defecating and urinating must be done some distance away from the trailer. It is not surprising that Romany tenants of official sites have no respect for the council-designed sheds that combine all the polluting activities of washing, laundering and defecating with the cooking facilities.

Gorgers take a different view. They don't separate the inner from the outer. They design and use kitchen sinks for multiple purposes. Hand soap can often be found next to a kitchen sink, alongside a dishcloth used for cleaning surfaces and the crockery. You'll never find this in a Romany caravan or trailer. Indeed, most don't have sinks at all.

Even the Romany view of domestic rubbish is at odds with that of the settled community. Gorger hygiene consists to some extent of containing, covering up or hiding dirt. There are often waste bins in every room. For Romany, trailers must not become a store of pollution. No waste bins are kept inside.

Attitudes to the disposing of rubbish outside vary according to the gypsy group, and to the people involved.

Permanent sites are generally clean; temporary sites don't have rubbish services. The gypsies and travellers living there know they're going to be moved on. Some don't see rubbish outside – so long as it's far away from the trailer – as a problem. Again, it is inner cleanliness that matters. Lurid before-and-after pictures of temporary gypsy or traveller sites do not show the interiors of the trailers, which are invariably dazzling displays of sparkling mirrors and ultra-clean china. As one Romany woman points out, 'People say we're dirty. I've seen houses with lovely tended front gardens, but you should have seen the dirt inside.'

Because settled people don't live by the same stringent cleanliness rules, gypsies take measures to ensure they aren't polluted by gorgers. If a gorger is offered tea in a gypsy trailer – an exceptional compliment – he or she may be served with a special cup, reserved for outsiders and considered unusable by the gypsy family. Many traditional Romany will not eat food prepared by gorger hands. They favour food in tins, packets or bottles to bread, pies or sandwiches made by gorgers.

Even the gypsy classification of animals is based on their rules regarding inner purity. Cats, rats, mice, dogs and foxes are all *mochadi*, or polluted, because they lick their fur, taking their hairs and outer-bodily dirt into their mouths and inner body. These animals also eat the inner and outer parts of smaller animals – more polluting still. Dogs retain some respect as hunters and protectors, but the cat is maligned and considered untouchable. Its regular washing – seen by gorgers as a sign of laudable cleanliness – is viewed by gypsies as shamefully dirty. Travellers express disgust that gorgers stroke cats and dogs, or allow their pets to lick human skin.

The horse (*grai*) is absolutely clean. It is not carnivorous and it does not lick its coat. It has other strengths. Culturally, the horse is an important mediator between gypsies and gorgers. Also, a horse is strong-willed. You can lead a horse to water but you cannot make it drink water that is impure. This chimes with the Romany.

However, head honcho is the hedgehog (*hotchi-witchi*). Its prickly exterior offers a rigid separation between its inner and outer self, and prevents self-grooming. To many Romany, hedgehog flesh is considered an almost sacred delicacy and an antidote to poisonous, or *mochadi*, substances within. Perhaps unsurprisingly, hedgehog liver is Romany caviar.

Ultimately, cleanliness is a cultural imperative to the Romany. It is easy to see why they might feel misunderstood.

'I don't see why gypsies do get the big bad name that they vandalise things and they mess everything up,' says Romany Clara Taylor, eighteen. 'Most travelling people are very clean and they get called "stinking gypsies". It is so wrong. I don't know where they get it from.'

Her dad, John, blames the usual suspects – politicians, residents' groups and the media. 'Every time they show you gypsies on the television, it is normally where there are some cars burned out. There is a lot of mess with big piles of rubbish everywhere. They paint them as people that are all bad. There are some bad amongst them – there is some bad in the world everywhere – but in general gypsies are people of a quiet nature that doesn't want all this violence and trouble and all this mess. They like to keep the place tidy. We'd like to be known as a traditional, friendly people that likes to travel about.'

John is particularly shocked by a recent headline in a local newspaper. 'It showed a photo of a site and it said, "Would you like these people to be parked next to you?" In black and white. I don't think people from other cultures would find it acceptable. If it said the same about a white man or a black man, there would be uproar about it.

'There are a lot of myths going around. They say, "Gypsies are all big thieves," in the media. "They steal your children." We have got plenty of children; we don't want to steal no more! We have got quite enough children of our own. We don't want to fight people. We don't want to burgle people. We are not trying to do that at all. We are just normal.'

John accepts that some gypsies and travellers are quicker to engage in violence with each other than gorgers. He insists that this is due to a different cultural outlook, nothing more. 'I mean, gypsies and travellers do have fights, but we don't just phone one another up and say, "I'll meet you up at the fair and we'll have a fight." It might be over a family feud or sometimes over a young man and woman who have split up or whatever.'

John says that the net result of public misconceptions about gypsies and travellers is that they have been forced to become insular. 'Gypsy people and travellers try to keep ourselves away from the public. It is not because we are frightened of the public, and it is not because we want the public to be frightened of us. It is because we know the public in general thinks we are all bad people.

'It has a lot to do with ourselves anyway, because we are

kind of secret, a secret culture; it has been for a long time. You wouldn't see members of the public coming to visit us much really, so they wouldn't see how we live. We don't make a big fuss about everything. We just live our own life and let everybody live theirs.'

John thinks gypsies need to fight back, to stand up and be counted. That's why he agreed to participate in *Big Fat Gypsy Weddings*: it's high time for a fair hearing.

'It's the only thing we can do to stop being pushed to the bottom of the pile,' says John. 'We want the public to see we're just normal people who happen to like moving about and who occasionally need a helping hand with our sick and with educating our kids, same as anyone else.'

> 'We are kind of secret, a secret culture; it has been for a long time. You wouldn't see members of the public coming to visit us much really, so they wouldn't see how we live.'

Traveller men are expected to provide a home for their family. Buying a caravan is the easy bit – a good-sized, habitable trailer can cost as little as £5,000. That's why some travellers have lots of disposable income: no mortgage. The real challenge is finding a place to put it. Of course, gypsies and travellers can't stop anywhere they like any more. They're fined, taken to court, ordered to move on. Councils are supposed to provide enough authorised sites to accommodate their traveller and gypsy populations. They don't.

As a result, traveller groups say that as many as 25,000 gypsies and travellers have no fixed place to live. Nineteen days after the last general election, a £50-million plan to construct traveller sites around London got scrapped. It's up to the traveller man to find somewhere safe and secure for his family to live. It's a task that's becoming harder and harder.

English traveller Swanley Smith, nineteen, lives at the Downs Caravan Site, near Caterham, Surrey. At six feet five and seventeen stone, nobody teases Swanley about his unusual name. Not that he'd mind. He's a mild-mannered, laid-back young man with brown hair and a pronounced jaw. He's like a baby-faced Russell Crowe, but broader and far more easy-going.

Swanley is taking us on a tour of the site where he's lived all his life. He knows everyone here because they're all family. Twenty-four years ago, the Smith clan pulled off the road for the last time and settled for the next best option – to live together in trailers on this pretty little site, tucked between the roaring M25 and the A22, south of London.

'On this site, it is all my family,' he says. 'You have got my grandfather and all his children and all his grandchildren. We all live here. Three generations.'

A close-knit community needs a place to socialise. Five years ago, Swanley and his pals built their very own social club. Swanley gives us a tour of its well-stocked bar, pool table, dartboard, tiny stage and collection of instruments. On the walls are DIY portraits of Hollywood greats.

'We hang out here in the evening, maybe have a few drinks, get a few people over. We have had some good times, some good laughs in this shed. My people love to sing and play. There's guitars, a piano, fiddles. We even have a little karaoke stage. We just love to have a good old singsong.'

Music, dancing and storytelling are gypsy traditions they're working hard to keep alive, because their biggest tradition – roaming in trailers – is dead. As a boy, Swanley got a brief taste of life on the road. Every summer his clan took their trailers off site to go touring. He loved it. Now this centuries-old travelling tradition has been killed off. 'You can't even go out for a weekend now,' he says. 'If you stop anywhere, you've got the police there straight away moving you on. It's just not worth the hassle.'

Since turning thirteen, Swanley's lived in his own trailer and earned his living as a manual worker and raising a few horses. He's happy to show off his piebalds, but not his trailer. 'I'd be too embarrassed. It's really scruffy,' he says.

In three weeks' time, Swanley marries Irish traveller Josie McFadden. So is this where he and Josie plan to live? For the first time today, the smile is wiped from Swanley's big, amiable face. He doesn't know where they are going to live yet. He's starting to feel the heat.

The newlyweds can't move in here. For one thing, there are no pitches left. But also, after twenty-four years, the site is being closed down. Council officials have detected methane gas leaks. Before it was home to the extended Smith clan, this was a landfill. Like many traveller sites, it is built on an old rubbish tip. Councils sure know how to make travellers feel loved.

So what now for the Smiths? 'We had a meeting about it

over a year ago and they said they'd get back to us in two weeks,' says Swanley. 'To date, they're about fifty weeks late. We don't know where we stand right now. You can't help thinking they sort their own kind out first.

'They reckon they are going to find somewhere else for us, but there's a chance they won't bother. I mean, everyone knows money is tight right now. Or they may offer us a piece of land so awful, next to a sewage works or something. In that case, we'll just have to go off and do our own thing.'

Swanley's options are limited, though. He and his family can't take to the road any more. All of Surrey County Council's pitches are occupied, with a waiting list. So where can they go? The Smiths could buy land and apply for planning permission to build a site. However, 90 per cent of gypsy and traveller planning applications are turned down. By contrast, just 10 per cent of the settled community is ever refused planning permission.

His relatives own some land down in Kent, but that's over a hundred miles from Josie's parents. She doesn't drive and can't stand the idea of being that far away. Of course, the other option is to move into a house. To someone like Swanley, who has lived his entire life in a trailer, moving into a house is the dreaded last resort. Swanley has only spent two nights in a house – his granny's – and it drove him crazy.

'I go over there for a couple of hours and then that is about it. I can't stand it any longer. I feel closed in. It's so hot. I just don't like them. It feels odd,' he says. 'For some reason, you just feel boxed in. When you are on a site, you can go off, and as soon as you walk out your trailer, you can call someone over and have a good old chat. You can have a laugh, have the craic. In a house, I feel too closed in.'

It might sound odd to settled people, but Swanley's fiancée, Josie, genuinely fears for his sanity living in a house. When he visits the McFadden home in Hillingdon, he suffers severe claustrophobia. 'If he's only a few hours in the house, he can't breathe. He feels like he's in a restraining jacket in a closet,' she says. 'It will be freezing and Swanley has gone and sneaked the heating off in the house. God only knows how he'd cope.'

Because he knows Josie is desperate to be close to her family, Swanley has gamely agreed to try living in a rented house somewhere in West London after they marry. They'll stay there at least until the situation with his family and the Downs Caravan Site has been sorted out. No matter what happens, though, it looks like the Smith clan – after twenty-four years living together – are breaking up. Swanley's going to miss his old life.

'Moving away from the family, I will be a bit bored, because at night you can just go over, knock all the boys up and drag them to the pub or even just have a chat and a laugh. Now, I'll be too far away. I can't drive all the way over there on the off chance of bumping into them. It's going to be lonely.'

Perhaps surprisingly, Swanley worries about the newly-weds being alone together in their new home. 'There'll be no one else to talk to except each other. Put bars on the window and it's a prison cell.'

'She's not a dog. She's not a dog. She's a human being. Who do they think they are?'

Thousands of travellers live their everyday lives in a Kafkaesque planning limbo. They accept that traditional life on the road is over. However, most travellers want to maintain their traditions by living together on caravan sites. Councils consistently fail to provide enough sites for travellers to pull onto.

Fair enough, some might say. Why should taxpayers' money be spent providing pitches for travellers? Travellers agree. They want to provide sites and pitches for themselves, but they find themselves in a catch-22, and it's happening all over Britain. What happens is that travellers and gypsies buy land to set up their own sites. When they seek planning permission to build a site, however, they are almost always turned down. It's the NIMBY (not in my back yard) factor; nobody wants gypsies or travellers living nearby. Out of desperation – they have to live somewhere, after all – travellers and gypsies have set up sites on land that they own, then sought retrospective planning permission. The flashpoint comes when retrospective planning permission is turned down, as it inevitably is. That makes the camp illegal. Councils are then under pressure from disgruntled neighbours, and often the local media, to clear these illegal encampments. The people on the site can expect twenty-eight days' notice to quit.

Across Britain, thousands of illegal traveller and gypsy

74

sites are awaiting the axe. Irish travellers have owned and occupied the Hovefields Site near Basildon, Essex, for twenty years. In August 2010, the fifty-plus residents received a notice to quit. They stayed.

★★
★★

It is a dark, wet September morning at Hovefields. Fifty bailiffs descend on the site in bright blue high-visibility jackets. They are backed up by trucks, cranes, three earth-movers and the local police.

In support of the Hovefields residents, a group of local non-travellers block the main entrance. One of them explains why. 'I mean, the travellers, some of them are anxious to move because this is a stressful situation to them, but they're all saying to me they have nowhere to move to. Do they park up on the side of the road? Do they go into a supermarket car park? What do they do?'

A tense stand-off lasts about an hour. Then, with little ceremony and less tact, the bailiffs move in on the protest-ors. They rip banners from their hands and set about dragging them away, one by one. The protestors sit down. A man in his fifties is hauled off through a puddle. A bailiff is yanking on the arms of a woman in her sixties. She says, 'Take your hands off me. You're bruising my arm.'

The bailiff responds, 'You don't have the right to stop this.'

The woman says, 'You're hurting me. Leave me alone.'

Another elderly woman is being hoisted away. She looks around, calling, 'No, no, I want the police here. Police!

Police!' But police officers are here. They're right behind her, looking on. One officer is busy filming the action.

For some traveller children, the sight of the elderly female protestor being pulled across hard, wet ground is too much. Sensing real fear for the first time, they scream, 'Let her go, let her go.'

A traveller woman, twenty-one-year-old Catherine McCann, has lived here with her entire family for six years. She speaks up, not about the imminent destruction of her own home, but about the oafish manhandling of this dignified lady.

'She's not a dog. She's not a dog. She's a human being. Who do they think they are? She's not an animal. She's human. I mean, come on, they've got the police here. The police is supposed to stop this.'

Two of the protestors are being arrested and led away. As soon as the last protestor is removed, an enormous yellow digger – with great caterpillar wheels and a protective metal frame around its front windscreen – thunders past. Inside the cab, dance music blares out of tinny speakers. Within seconds, the mobile disco has turned a prefab building to mulch. It charges on hungrily towards a flimsy shed.

Grattan Puxon, founder of the Gypsy Council, tells the assembled media, 'We want a response from Eric Pickles, the communities minister, who has been asked by the UN Commission for the Elimination of Racial Discrimination to halt these evictions. They haven't been halted.'

Perched on a six-foot wooden perimeter fence, a young boy in a bright red T-shirt watches his village getting smashed to bits. Jerry Cassidy has red hair and a wise, worried face. He shelters from the drizzle beneath his mum's pink flowery umbrella.

Jerry's asked why he thinks this is happening. 'It's because they don't like gypsies, do they? They don't like travellers.'

He's asked if he's ever seen anything like this before. Jerry says, 'Once or twice, but I only got a little glimpse. But this is much worse. I've never seen diggers this size in my life. And it's very horrific . . . You don't want a child to be seeing all this, like a baby or a two-, three-year-old. They'd be seeing all this thinking, What's going on?'

Jerry believes he's old enough to cope with watching his home being destroyed by bailiffs. 'I am old enough,' he says firmly. 'I'm twelve, coming on thirteen.'

Amid the destruction, one campaigner who's witnessed dozens of traveller evictions expresses surprise. 'They're being careful today because the media is here. We've got footage of people being beaten to the floor, wheelchairs burning on bonfires, children's toys being thrown on bonfires in front of them. We've got footage of one woman who was trying to get her child and an eight-month-old baby from a trailer, screaming, hysterical and heavily pregnant, asking to go back in to get them. One bailiff says, "If we let her back in, she might not come out again." The bailiffs held her back while one of them went in and took the children out.'

The only reported casualty today is a seventy-year-old resident, who suffers a broken nose.

By evening time, three families have pulled off Hovefields. Four stay on. The next morning, as the machines continue their orgy of destruction, police deliver an ultimatum to the remaining travellers: leave by midday or else. They pull off mid-morning. Later that day, the four families stop at a nearby car park. The police turn up and move them on using Section 60 of the Criminal Justice Act 1994, which prohibits the gathering of more than six vehicles. They spend that night at South Mimms Services.

Like thousands of other travellers and gypsies, they have no idea where to go next. One thing they can be certain of: there is no healthcare or regular education for kids on the road.

CHAPTER FOUR

Kiss and Tell

'They have got to try and stand out to bag a husband.'

The social life of a single traveller girl revolves around the milestones in the lives of her family and friends – christenings, Communions and, especially, weddings. A wedding represents her best chance of meeting a future husband. Travellers' big, brash, bacchanalian wedding receptions are fertile breeding grounds for fresh couplings. Many of the *BFGW* couples met at a wedding.

One gorger woman has been to more traveller weddings than any other. Dressmaker Thelma Madine declares, 'You haven't lived until you've been to a traveller wedding.'

The craic starts in the church. For reasons that no one is willing to explain, most of the men spend the ceremony hanging about near the entrance, chatting. Inside, the anticipation is electric. Not so much about the nuptials. Everyone here has been to loads of weddings. They know the words off by heart! The buzz is all about the bride's dress. What will she be wearing? Virtually every traveller bride tries to come up with an original twist or theme for her dress, and for those of her bridesmaids, who normally number between five and nine. These themes are as diverse as the girls getting wed: butterflies, tropical, flamenco, Wild West, Snow White, Princess and the Frog, swans, flowers . . . Other brides want trophy dresses: the biggest, the longest, the heaviest, the shiniest – Thelma's designed them all.

When the bride appears, the congregation turns as one to eyeball her creation. This is the day's headline. Breaking news.

Often, the bride is more flushing than blushing. Thelma's heavyweight numbers can weigh in at anything between fourteen and twenty stones. What's behind the bride can be even more astounding. The latest must-have is a mini-bride – a young girl dressed in an identical outfit to the bride. And yes, they have mini-grooms too.

As the ceremony begins, it's far from pin-drop quiet. People natter away merrily all through the service. The kids do what they want.

Thelma recalls one particularly laid-back, finger-lickin' service. 'We've been to a wedding service where they've gone to the Kentucky and come back and sat and had their Kentucky while the wedding is going on, so everybody just does what they want.'

Once the 'I do's are out of the way, the pumpkin carriage awaits Cinderella, invariably with a modern twist. *BFGW* couples have been spirited to and from their ceremonies in

Hummers, Rollers, limos, a helicopter, as well as in horse-drawn Victorian carriages. Older guests marvel at the irony – the horse and wagon, which is now a novelty, was, two generations back, a part of everyday life for them.

Everyone speculates as to what might come next. As one wedding veteran says, 'The only thing I haven't seen yet is a hot-air balloon, a boat or a jet – and I stress *yet*.'

Any traveller is welcome to the reception – there's no guest list. Travellers come from all over the country. Clocking up big mileage to make a do is a major show of respect to the bride's family.

Dining is a free-for-all. Thelma again: 'First time you go, it's a real eye-opener. You walk in and go, "Wow!" When someone is telling you at a wedding to run as fast as you can when the doors open and put your ass on a seat, then you think, What's all this about? You realise that's just the way they are. There's nothing uniform about them. There's nobody saying, "Be upstanding for the bride and groom," and everyone's sat in their right little place. That doesn't happen.'

Then it's time for the first dances. A traveller bride doesn't have just one wedding dance with her new husband; she has a series of individual dances with those closest to her. The first dance is usually with her dad, the second with her mum and so on. The bride has hand-picked a song for each dance that she feels says what she wants to say. Because every traveller bride is leaving her home and her family – often for the first time – these wedding dances can be the emotional climax of the day.

Next comes the gender split. At every traveller wedding, the men cluster at one end – normally next to the bar

– while girls and women flock around the dance floor. No one knows why this custom is in place, or why it is so rigidly observed. Then the peacocks go to work on the dance floor. According to Thelma, the girls aren't just under social pressure to hook a husband in their teens; there is an additional biological burden.

'The traveller community is predominantly women,' she says. 'There is a lot more women than men.' There are several theories about why this imbalance exists. Gypsy men tend to marry settled girls more often than gypsy girls marry out. They also emigrate more than girls and have a lower life expectancy. The girls are conditioned from six and seven to be a homemaker, so they have got to find a husband. From the day they can understand, their thing in life is to get a husband. That's the way they are going to get looked after, because they don't work. If they are not married by the time they are twenty-one or twenty-two, they are basically on the shelf. So they have got to look the best. It is like peacocks on parade. The best one is going to get chosen.

Competition is fierce. It isn't enough for traveller girls to look sexy. They must *show* sexy.

'They dance as provocatively as they possibly can to make them stand out from the rest, because every one of them young girls in there looks good. How else are they going to attract a man? They have got to try and stand out to bag a husband.'

Thelma knows that if a girl danced in such a sexual way in a high-street nightclub, everyone there would assume she was 'easy'. At a traveller wedding, it means nothing of the sort. The girl will leave as she arrived – with her parents.

'Putting it crudely, they are showing their wares and what they have got, but it is look but don't touch.'

According to Paddy Doherty, travellers try not to fight at weddings. 'You don't want to spoil the day. People say stupid things when they're drunk, so you try to walk away. Take it up with them the next morning. You say, "Listen, me and you had a few words last night. I want to fight you. I'll fight you now." The man says, "No, I'll fight you in six weeks. Get yourself ready. We'll fight win, lose or draw." When they finish the fight, they will go to the pub and get drunk with you. And that's what you call a good sportsman.'

Fights break out at a couple of the upcoming big fat gypsy weddings. One of them even has to end prematurely. But, as Thelma points out, that happens at gorger weddings too. 'In Liverpool, they used to say a wedding isn't a good wedding without a fight. I think I've seen trouble at a traveller wedding once, maybe twice.'

Thelma says that readers should focus instead on how good travellers are at enjoying themselves. 'One thing settled people can learn from the travellers is how to throw a party. Whether it's a christening, an engagement, a wedding, they are just mad! I mean, ours are boring compared to theirs.'

'I would wear it once. That is it. Once and then goodbye. That is the dress gone. It would just be hanging up in the cupboard.'

On a midweek afternoon in Walton-on-Thames, West London, fifteen-year-old traveller cousins Cheyenne and Montana Pidgley are on a vital mission. Cheyenne is the drily funny, style-conscious blonde who dresses to impress. Today, she's dressed down in denim shorts, large white belt and cropped white top. Montana's positively slumming it in a functional yellow vest and shorts. Both mean business.

On Saturday, the girls are going to Josie McFadden's wedding evening. For traveller girls and boys, weddings are the mainstay of their social calendar, and their best chance for romance.

'Any wedding that comes up, we are always there,' says Montana, 'and there is a wedding normally about every week or at least once a month. Even if we don't know them, we still go anyway. Travellers don't mind how many turns up. They say the more the merrier. Every time we find out about one, we always end up going to meet new people.'

It's approaching June and the girls have already attended 'about twelve' weddings this year. Montana explains what makes a good one. 'My favourite wedding would be a rough-and-ready one because you meet new people, and even if you don't know the boys and girls, they would just grab you by the hand and say, "Come and dance!" and that way you meet new people all of the time.'

For 'meet new people' read 'meet potential boyfriend/ husband'. Again, though, Prince Charming isn't the over-riding reason for attending all these weddings. They want to keep an eye on the competition. One thing is certain: the fathers of these fifteen-year-old cousins won't be giving their girls away cheaply.

'One girl, she had a very good wedding,' gushes Cheyenne. 'She had singers there, she spent over sixty-five thousand on flowers, and she had water fountains, ice statues. She even had an ice-cream van there, and she had Stacey Solomon there. She had a big marquee in the back of her garden with a big projector screen. She had everything that a girl could dream of for a wedding.'

Cheyenne and Montana are rifling through a snazzy little boutique called Pink Ice. The girls don't do high-street chains.

'Some girls buy cheap dresses out of River Island or somewhere like that and get loads of diamonds and sparkle put on them,' says Montana. 'Then when you say, "Where did you get your dress from?" they say, "I don't know!" or, "I can't tell you." Well, they won't tell you anyway. I would never get a dress from River Island.'

Cheyenne agrees. 'No way,' she sniffs. 'It's just not special, is it? It is just River Island. It's cheap. These dresses are more classy.'

This is the first stop on what could prove an exhaustive whistle-stop tour of London boutiques. They won't rest until they've hunted down exactly the right outfits.

'I did get this dress off the Internet,' says Montana. 'It come today, but it is no good. I just don't like it. I tried it on and it is just not my thing.' Montana's thinking bling. 'I want an outstanding dress if I can get one. One with loads of diamonds on it, really sparkly.'

Cheyenne explains that – like many traveller girls – she too suffers Cinderella syndrome. 'It is all about looking the best and impressing. Just to feel good in yourself, because all through the week you don't really dress up. You are just in a tracksuit or something like that, just to clean up in. So when it comes to a wedding, you have to make the most of it.'

The girls are determined to play a starring role in the wedding evening's dance-floor spectacle. They know what they'll be up against. 'I don't think we will see many long dresses there,' says Cheyenne, powder-dry, 'and if we do, they'll have splits up to the waist. I think the girls there will be wearing tutu dresses. Or, like, just really little outfits. Or a corset and skirt. All very small.'

They've comprehensively sacked and plundered every rail in the boutique to no avail. 'I think we should go to the dressmaker's, get something made,' suggests Cheyenne. 'It is important to have a dress that nobody else has had. I have never turned up in the same dress as another girl. Montana has.'

Montana reddens at the recollection. 'My brown-and-gold tutu dress with the sequins on top! Charlene had it on too! I was ashamed to death.'

The girls have one golden rule when it comes to wedding outfits – never wear the same thing twice.

'Like every time there is a wedding, a dance, you always buy a new dress,' says Cheyenne. 'It does get expensive, but what can you do? If you need a new dress, then you need a new dress. A new dress for each occasion.'

So how costly is this 'one do, one dress' rule? 'The most I have ever spent is three hundred pounds,' Cheyenne announces casually. 'Then you've got to get the shoes, get your hair done. If I liked the dress, I couldn't care about

Traveller girls strut their stuff

Cousins Cheyenne and Montana

Cheyenne being 'grabbed' at a wedding

A traveller girl interupts a game of pool

Carrying this spectacular wedding
cake is a three-person job!

Lizzie Lee cleaning
her family's trailer

Lizzie Lee, touching
up her make-up on
her wedding day

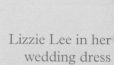

Lizzie Lee in her
wedding dress

Violet Anne working at the hotel reception

Violet Anne's dad, Bill

Violet Anne on her wedding day

Young Bridget on her way to the church

Young Bridget being helped out of her carriage by her parents. Her dress weighs over 7 stone

Sam's butterfly dress in all its glowing glory

Bridget Doran at the altar

Bridget Doran with her mother. Bridget senior escaped
her violent marriage and became one of the first
traveller women to divorce

Bridget on her daughter's
wedding day

Bridget at the wedding
reception, after catching her
daughter's bouquet

the price. I would pay up to three hundred and fifty. I deserve it. I have to clean up. I have to make all the beds, wash up. Just do all of the cleaning, anything my mum asks me to do. My mum and dad have never said no to buying a dress. I would wear it once. That is it. Once and then goodbye. That is the dress gone. It would just be hanging up in the cupboard.'

Cheyenne spells out why wearing a dress a second time is not an option. 'Because people have seen you in it. It don't feel the same if you wear the same dress over and over again. It doesn't feel as nice as the time you first wore it. And people see you in the same old dress. If I saw a person in the same old dress, you think, Oh, here she comes again, in her dress.'

'As long as there's a Planet Earth, Appleby Fair will exist. They'll never get rid of this one.'

Traveller romances aren't just ignited at weddings. Many married couples first meet at one of the annual historic horse fairs, which attract gypsies and travellers in their thousands. The biggest is Appleby Horse Fair in Cumbria, which draws 10,000 gypsies and travellers, and twice that number of curious country people. King James II granted a royal charter for the fair back in 1685, which means it can't be banned by the authorities, unlike many other historic horse fairs.

'As long as there's a Planet Earth, Appleby Fair will

exist. They'll never get rid of this one. We wouldn't allow it. We would literally lay our lives down for it. It's that important to us,' says fair organiser and Romany leader Billy Welch. 'We don't get classed as citizens in our own country, so we don't really feel that we belong anywhere, but we feel we belong here. This place is sacred to us. It is literally our Mecca.'

Pilgrims to Appleby Fair are treated to sights as old as the event itself. Two men clasp their spit-soaked hands together, sealing their horse deal. A brown-faced matriarch traces an outstretched palm with her long, searching fingers, practising the ancient craft of *dukkeripen*, or fortune-telling. An ad hoc pitch-and-toss school sees knots of men bet frenziedly. Transfixed tourists watch traveller kids riding their steeds bareback along the country roads, or skilfully guiding them across the stiff currents of the town's River Eden. The procession up Fair Hill is an unruly cavalcade of carts and caravans, flanked by dappled cobs, cross-breeds, thoroughbreds and New Forest ponies.

The campsites tell of more recent history. The gaily decorated wooden Romany *vardo* wagons – those bow-topped cocoons with their gilded carvings and vibrant arabesques – are out in force. A surprisingly large number seem to have escaped the scrapyard, the woodworm and the weather. They are dwarfed by spacious, modern trailers fitted with gas bottles, washing machines and satellite dishes.

In this gypsy and traveller Mecca, one unlikely spot is considered the Holy Land by single boys and girls: the town's NCP car park. Here, another timeless ritual is conducted. Girls in packs strut their stuff in tight dresses, bra tops, tiny shorts, corsets and tutu skirts. Taking in the style is a woman fêted like a celebrity in these circles, dress-maker Thelma Madine.

'I'd say the main style of the outfits today is, like, really short skirts, thigh-high boots, belly tops. I don't think it's fake tan, I think it's basically sunbeds, but they're all brown. They've all got hair extensions and really high thigh-high boots, covered in Swarovski diamonds or crystal. Again, everything is bling; everything is designed to stand out.'

Boys lean against their cars and vans, trying to look nonchalant but taking in the sights. Perched above it all on a wall with a grandstand view, Martin Tom Doherty, Davey McDonagh and their pal Asa eye the girls ravenously, as a fox might a brood of hens. All three sport perfectly coif-fured hair. Uniform vests showcase their topped-up tans.

There's no feigned nonchalance up here. 'Aren't they the best women you have ever clocked in your lives?' says a thunderstruck Martin Tom, to no one in particular.

A year ago, Asa met his girlfriend, Leanne, at Appleby Fair. Asa is an English traveller. Tall, fair, with pronounced teeth, a lean face and good skin, he's one of those good-looking but gawky young men yet to grow into his face and body. From looking at him, you'd never think he's a traveller.

With a year's 'courting' under his belt, Asa can reveal the etiquette of traveller dating – the unwritten rules of travel-ler romance – from a boy's point of view.

'When you start to go out with a girl,' he explains, 'you don't really want her dad to know, do you? Not at the start. If her dad knows, you think, Oh my God! And then you'll go out with a girl for a while. Then, if you like her, you'll ask for her. Irish people just ask to marry the girls; they don't tend to ask to court them.

'But, like, English boys, we'll go to the father, to the girl-friend's dad, and say, "Can I court your daughter?" I asked Leanne's father. He said, "Yeah," and that was it. But, like, now I can go inside her house, so it's like another home, sort of thing. I see her, like, once a week, or twice, three times even.'

There is one overriding, *numero uno* law of traveller romance – no sex. Or anything else, beyond kissing.

'Me and my girlfriend's, like, eleven months now . . . All I've done is kiss her. Eleven month . . . that's like a long time, nearly for a year sort of thing, and all I've done is kiss her! There's boys and girls going out two years, three year, and it's like the girl still won't chance doing anything because if he finishes it, that's it. That's her name gone! Girls think a lot of their name.'

Davey explains that traveller girls in long-term relation-ships – even engaged – have to preserve their God-given good name. He says, 'If a girl does things with a boy before she gets married, they get a bad name for themselves. Every girl out there tries to keep her name. Just kissing, kissing, that's it!'

Surely, as they watch these lithe and pretty girls go past, the boys envy the sex on offer to their settled counterparts? The boys deliver a resounding and uniform no. They insist they wouldn't change a thing. They're perfectly happy to stay chaste until marriage.

'It's a cleaner way of living,' says Davey, 'and it shows the respect we have for our women.'

Not all traveller women command manly respect. At

Appleby, Martin Tom and Davey will be on red alert for a dangerous minority: the number-plate girls.

Davey explains, 'Some girls are called like "number-plate girls", where they go for, like, the reg of your motor. It's what they go for, like, a nice motor. If you have a top-of-the-range car, then they're like, "I'll go for you."'

'Believe me,' adds Martin, with a knowing nod, 'I only get number-plate girls.' Martin Tom doesn't own a car. However, his daddy acquires a brand-new motor every six months. Intelligence about such family wealth goes viral on the traveller grapevine.

'Like some husbands beat their wives — they hit them and don't think anything of it, but not every husband. Some husbands do, some husbands don't. You have got to find the good ones from the bad ones.'

In leafy Walton-on-Thames, South-West London, sits a tiny two-berth caravan with the somewhat grandiose model name 'Challenger'. The only thing this titchy trailer has in common with the space shuttle is that it's white and it's cramped inside. This is home to South London style queen Cheyenne Pidgley. Her dress collection would most likely topple over her little residence. The Imelda Marcos range – as her dad calls it – has been airlifted from chez Cheyenne into the family home, to fill a spare bedroom.

Inside the Challenger, Cheyenne is jockeying for space in front of a tiny make-up mirror with her best pal, Montana, who lives with her family in a house nearby. All eight square metres of the trailer is Cheyenne chic. Pink cushions. Porcelain dolls. Coloured glass vases. Make-up cases. A scattering of jewellery boxes.

Josie McFadden's nuptials are fast approaching, so the big question is, have these indefatigable fashionistas found their fairy-tale frocks for the wedding?

'I bought two dresses,' says Cheyenne. 'One was from Pink Ice and one was from Fonthill Road in London. Montana got her dress made in a shop there. The one I'm wearing is a black tutu dress that comes out and then it has a few diamonds at the bottom, sequin things at the top. Then some diamond shoes and diamond earrings to match it and then . . . add accessories.'

Montana had wanted bling; she got it. Her outfit is 'a gem'. 'My dress is red and comes to above my knee. There's lots of gems on it, and it has red gloves with gems on it and red matching shoes with all gems on them.'

Knockout frocks. Killer peacock chic. But for what? At fifteen, the girls say they aren't allowed to have a boyfriend. They must be sixteen – and even then, they can't go out with a boy alone. To make matters more complicated, both have been asked out by boys they like. They said no. They had to say no. Obeying the rules pays for those frocks.

'I have been asked to go to the pictures with a boy, but I never have,' explains Cheyenne. 'I have always turned them down because I am too young. I will go to the pictures with a boy when I'm sixteen, but only if it is someone I liked. I wouldn't go to the pictures with someone for the sake of it.' No film is worth that.

Although they're not allowed to date boys yet, the girls know the mating rituals, the unwritten rules for girls. Dating, it seems, has a bewildering statute book of 'do's and don'ts' all of its own.

For example, traveller girls don't do restaurants. 'Not a lot of travelling girls like to eat in front of the boys,' says Cheyenne. 'I really wouldn't like to eat in front of a boy, no way. Sitting there like a big pig! Can you imagine it? I will have this. I will have that. If a boy offered me a drink, I am not ashamed to say yes, but Montana would say, "No, I am fine," even if she's dying of thirst. But me, I would say yeah. If I need a drink, I need a drink.'

'I'd be too ashamed,' says Montana.

Under the rules of traveller romance, even agreeing to date a boy is a protracted and unfathomable process.

Cheyenne does her best to make sense of it. 'If a boy liked me, he would find out my number, he would call me and ask about his chances. You would give him his chances and he would ask you out. If he asks you out, you wouldn't say yes straight away, and then they would ask you and ask you and ask you out, and eventually you would say OK, and you would go to the pictures or something like that. A boy has got to ask you out for a good month.'

As, astronaut style, they make their final checks in the Challenger pre-take-off, the girls talk about the kind of husband they want. They are far less certain about this than they are about the style and design of their wedding dresses. It's worth remembering that Montana plans to marry at seventeen or eighteen, Cheyenne at sixteen. Just as well the fifteen-year-olds know at least roughly what they're looking for. Or rather what they don't want . . .

Montana goes first. 'I would like a man that doesn't lie in bed all day, goes to work, gives you money, that is nice to you, doesn't go off to the pub every night, shows that they care, don't go off to nightclubs, don't go off with other women. Be just like your man. Don't beat you up. Like some husbands beat their wives – they hit them and don't think anything of it, but not every husband. Some husbands do, some husbands don't. You have got to find the good ones from the bad ones.'

Cheyenne has her own checklist for Prince Charming. 'I would like a very loyal husband that stood by you everywhere you walked and protected you, but it is quite hard to find one of them.'

Montana is confident: 'Don't worry, I will find one.'

Cheyenne less so: 'Hopefully I will find one too.'

'Girls won't give you a kiss straight away, so you got to, kind of, beat them for the kiss. You gotta work for a kiss, man – you gotta bend its arm, you gotta punch for a kiss.'

The unwritten rules governing the single traveller girls featured on *BFGW* can be broken down as follows:

You can't go to pubs, clubs or anywhere that country people might lurk.

You cannot talk to, let alone date, a country boy.

You must leave school before age thirteen.

You must only attend traveller or gypsy events.

You can't go out anywhere without the company of family or friends.

You cannot date a boy until you're sixteen without Dad's permission.

You cannot marry a boy without Dad's permission.

You can only see your traveller boyfriend in the company of others.

You cannot engage in anything sexual with any boy, other than kissing, until marriage.

The traveller Nine Commandments obviously don't apply to all gypsy and traveller girls, but they apply to many of the girls we spoke to – and they say they are happy to comply. However, there's a custom within the Irish traveller community that circumvents quite a few of these unwritten rules. Indeed, some say this is exactly why it has developed. It is known as 'grabbing' or 'grabs', and it's pretty much exactly as it sounds. *Big Fat Gypsy Weddings* first learns about grabbing at the Appleby Horse Fair, thanks to those teenage 1950s throwbacks Martin Tom Doherty and his cousin and pal Davey McDonagh.

Firstly, Davey explains that single traveller boys come to Appleby for the grab. 'Years ago, men came to Appleby Fair for the horses. Now it's for the women. If you come to Appleby and don't grab a woman, there's something wrong with you. No matter where you go in Appleby, there is women! There's about five girls to every boy.'

When they're asked to explain 'grabbing', Martin Tom and Davey shift uncomfortably. They realise it will seem alien to settled society, but they have promised to be completely honest and frank about their lives. Now, to their credit, they honour that promise. At first, though, Martin Tom exaggerates. He's deliberately trying to shock.

He goes on to explain, tongue planted firmly in cheek, 'Grabbing is where you get a girl and literally make her give you a kiss. Girls won't give you a kiss straight away, so you got to, kind of, beat them for the kiss. You gotta work for a kiss, man – you gotta bend its arm, you gotta punch for a kiss. Basically, there's no better way to put it, is there? There's no friendly way in putting it!'

As if on cue, a girl is 'grabbed' in Appleby car park. It is as swiftly executed as it is shocking. The boy grabs her round her waist, lifts her off her feet and hoists her like a side of meat towards a secluded alleyway. All the while, she screams, struggles, scratches and screams some more, but in Appleby, no one hears you scream. Grab a horse? You'll get beaten to death. Grab a single girl and run off with her? Fair play to you! You've just engaged in the Irish traveller trend of 'grabbing'. No one follows them to the alleyway to check that she's OK. That would be plain rude.

Davey explains the tactics employed. 'You ask them for

a walk first, they say no, and then you get them and drag them away. And obviously, they don't walk away with you. You have to drag them on.'

Martin Tom picks it up. 'I ask them – don't get me wrong. I have beat girls for kisses. You ask them nicely for about ten minutes. If they don't, you start to bend their arm or pull their finger and they're bound to give in!'

Tommy Sharp, another cousin, known to all as 'Mush', is on hand with his input. 'Every travelling boy grabs girls.'

The boys insist that despite the aggression employed, they don't hurt girls when they grab them.

'I think hitting a girl when you're grabbing her makes no sense at all,' says Martin Tom. 'No sense. Fair enough, like, an arm twist, but I haven't hit a girl grabbing. First-class wrong; boys shouldn't hit a girl. End of story. Boys grabbing, punching and pulling girls' hair and ripping them, that's wrong. It truly is.'

'I agree,' says Davey. 'I haven't, like, beat a girl up. I haven't done that.'

They know boys who do, although these stories are clearly the exception rather than the rule.

'One man I know, Tony, he's a brutal fellow when it comes to grabbing, especially when he's drunk, isn't he?' says Martin Tom. Grave nods all round. 'I don't think there is anyone like him. He gets them and then he punches them, punches them again. Oh, man, he's just one of them thick people. All to get a kiss. He will get a kiss no matter what it takes.'

Davey has seen it too. 'You can get some that literally drag them away and punch them in the face and near break their arm, like, behind their back. I've seen a girl getting grabbed off a dance floor from the top of the head, like. I've seen girls running, like, trying to run away from getting grabbed, then fall upside down. The man just get them by the head and drag them outside. Country people, they'd get you done for sexual and physical assault, trust me, for what these fellers do.'

However, both lads are quick to point out that most travellers are much more chivalrous, and that they've seen rowdy country boys behaving just as badly.

The boys say grabbing is acceptable, yet each then says he would fight anyone who grabbed their sister. Heaven help the brotherless traveller girl.

'Seriously,' says Martin Tom, 'if I saw my sister getting grabbed – no point in lying – I'd go over and I'd sort it out a million per cent, and if it did turn into a fight, then, fuck it, what can you do? A million per cent I'd be over there like a bullet.'

Traveller girls can't be seen to be an 'easy grab'. They tend to fight their grabbers tooth and nail, and then with anything else they can get hold of, including stiletto heels. The boys like it that way.

'She can't give in too easy,' explains Martin Tom, ''cos if you give in too easy, you're known as an easy grab, an easy kiss, and that's a name you don't want either.'

Once a traveller boy has dragged his victim to a quiet spot, the next challenge is getting that all-important kiss. It doesn't tend to run as smoothly as, say, a candlelit dinner and roses, but then the girl isn't allowed out for a candlelit dinner with a boy – even if he turns up with flowers.

'It's very awkward,' says Martin Tom. 'Like, some girls might say, "Look, you're not getting a kiss, end of story,' and five minutes down the line, boom, they're kissing you. It's all how you grab them, if you ask me. If you grab them, like, punching them and grabbing their hair and doing all of that, they won't kiss you.'

Davey, as usual, has it all figured out. 'If the girl likes you, she'll give you a kiss. If she doesn't, she won't, will she? You can tell the first two or three minutes if they're going to give you a kiss.'

Although there's no arguing with Davey's grabbing logic, he hasn't accounted for overweening male traveller pride. Failure to get a kiss after a grab equals humiliation. Losing a straight gender dual raises question marks about your manliness, from boys and girls.

As Mush puts it, 'If you be failed, that's bad. That's the worst thing that can happen. It's good for the girl and bad for the boy. It's shameful.'

However, Martin Tom – ever the traveller gent – sees it somewhat differently. 'Like, in a way, if I did get a kiss, I wouldn't say anything anyway,' he says. 'Just to know that I got one would be very good. Like, I'm not really one of those fellers who goes back to the boys and says, "Oh, I got a kiss off her." There's no point, like, because then the girl's never going to give you a kiss again. So if you like the girl, you're not going to tell no one, even if the boys are making a laugh of you. As long as you know you got a kiss . . .'

The boys insist that, during the course of a grab, they seek a kiss only, nothing more. The caveman manoeuvre is, it seems, underpinned by an almost Victorian chivalry.

'Just a kiss,' confirms Martin Tom. 'If you ask for something else, you're just dirty, aren't you? That shouldn't even come into your head, if you ask me. If you do that to a travelling girl, that's just dirty. It's . . . rough.'

What do the boys think traveller girls make of being grabbed? Here, Martin Tom and Davey are again at odds.

Martin Tom says, 'I don't think a girl will enjoy a grab unless she likes the boy really, but I doubt it very much otherwise.'

Davey disagrees. 'They think nothing of it! They know it's coming. Whoever's walking round, they know that they might get grabbed. It's up to themselves really then. If they're gonna put themselves on show, they're gonna get grabbed. Some girls like it, honest to God.'

Martin Tom concedes the point. 'Some girls do want to get grabbed. There is no point lying. Some girls will throw you a hint, or some girls will say something, or you can tell by the way they act around you. But most of the time girls don't want to get grabbed.'

The boys know that they could never grab a country girl from the settled community. 'You'd be done for rape or something,' says Martin Tom. 'Can you imagine? They'd be an outcry.'

While they accept that settled society might find the whole custom of grabbing girls intolerable, Martin says it's wrong for outsiders to judge. 'Every religion has their own ways,' Martin Tom points out. 'Like travellers have their own ways about grabbing and like other religions have weird things to which we go, like, "Oh my God, how could you do that?" That's their way. Who are we to question their way, and who are they to question our way?'

> 'It can really hurt, especially when they twist your arm around, pull your head back. I've seen girls in pain many times. I have seen them crying.'

That's the teen traveller-boy view on grabbing, but what do the girls think? Although grabbing is hardly an everyday occurrence in the gypsy and traveller communities, we found that the *BFGW* girls have their own take on the issue.

English Cinderellas Cheyenne and Montana Pidgley are on their way to the ball, in ladybird red and black. They suspect there will be grabs at Josie McFadden's wedding, as there are at many Irish traveller dos. Though the custom is unique to Irish travellers, the boys are happy to grab traveller girls of any origin!

Cheyenne says, 'Yeah, like, grabbing or grabs is very well known. You will see it a lot at weddings – boys dragging girls by their hair, dragging them by their waist. A boy will grab a girl, take a girl off and they will say, "Will you give us a kiss?" And the girl can say yes or no. I say no.

'You just keep saying no, no, no, no, and they would just keep hurting you. It can really hurt, especially when they twist your arm around, pull your head back. I've seen girls in pain many times. I have seen them crying. Screaming. Some girls lay it on, I think.'

When a girl is grabbed, there's nothing any of her friends

can do to help her. As Montana explains, 'If you go to help a girl, the boy says, "I'll get you grabbed in a minute, so if I was you, I would go away." So you can't help your friends or nothing.'

What happens if the boy has pushed all the pain-threshold buttons and still fails to get the kiss? Cheyenne says she has been there. 'If you still won't give them a kiss after all that, they've failed. But boys don't like to fail. They hope to get a kiss at the end of it because otherwise they have made themselves look like idiots.'

'Some are very stubborn,' explains Montana. 'They don't like to be called a failure. They'll have you standing there for hours. They don't like the shame to walk back and say, "No, never got it. I never got a kiss."'

What does it mean to a girl when a boy grabs them, kiss or no kiss?

'That means they like a girl,' says Cheyenne, 'or they think that they are good-looking. It means they want to get to know them and get their number.'

Montana says young Irish traveller men think grabbing is the only way they can get to know a girl. 'The Irish guys believe that you grab them, ask them for a kiss and then they might give you a kiss. They might give you their number. I think that they believe that is how to show a girl that they like them.'

According to Cheyenne and Montana, a lot of girls accept grabbing as a part of the courting ritual. Some girls, they say, even like it.

'Some of the Irish girls accept it. They believe that it is how you meet a boy, but then some don't. Some English girls accept it too. Everyone is different. Some girls like getting grabbed. They love it.'

Cheyenne and Montana say they don't like grabs one bit.

'That is just not the way I would like to meet a boy,' says Cheyenne. 'I don't believe in grabs, but you can't help that you are grabbed, like you don't choose to get grabbed.'

The girls reveal their tried-and-tested tactic to thwart a would-be grabber: 'If you say, "My dad is over there!" they get off you and they run,' giggles Cheyenne, 'but if you want to avoid getting grabbed, it is best to stay inside. Don't walk outside or you'll get grabbed for sure.'

The grabbing of young women is, to some, an accepted part of Irish traveller life. Small wonder, then, that Cheyenne and Montana report a general lack of respect for girls among traveller boys.

Cheyenne says, 'There are a few boys that aren't respectful.'

Montana puts it far more strongly. 'There is more of that kind than respectful boys! There are some real pests. They will rip your hair in front of all of the boys, just to look like the man by ripping a girl's hair. Or some boys punch you. They punch you in the arm like that or pull your hair because they think that is flirting, but it is not. It really hurts. They keep ripping your hair like this when you're dancing to get you to turn around. It is maybe to make themselves look big, but really it makes them look very small.'

Both girls look forward to having a boyfriend, if only for protection.

'The girls will bring you to one side and say, "I want a grabbing outfit." That basically means that they want to find a husband.'

It's Saturday morning at Appleby Fair. Martin Tom and Davey wake up after a bad night's sleep in Asa's car. While Davey sprays on deodorant, Martin Tom eats a cereal bar and tries to fix his coiffure. Both boys look considerably less slick than they did twelve hours earlier. Unwell, almost.

Martin Tom looks underwhelmed by his night's score. 'I grabbed one girl, got two or three numbers, got a kiss, so it wasn't too bad. What about you, Davey? How did you get on?'

Davey shrugs. 'Same as him really, just two or three numbers. Got a grab. That's it really. Good enough really.'

Martin Tom still seems unhappy with his tally. 'It's all right. It's not the greatest. You could do better, but it's better than getting nowt, isn't it? That's the way I look at it!'

Although grabbing might look decidedly 'caveman' to someone from the settled community, travellers under-stand why it goes on in their culture; many argue that, in a roundabout way, it's all to do with the stringent unwritten rules imposed on young single girls. If a girl fancies a boy, how can she get to know him? She can't approach a boy – she has to wait for him to make the first move. She's not allowed to be alone with him. If she's under sixteen, they can't date, even in company. However, if a girl is grabbed, everyone in the community accepts that she can do little about it, except try to resist. As long as the grabbed girl puts up a decent fight, she is no danger of losing her good name or getting scandalised.

As Martin Tom Doherty says, a boy only grabs a girl if he knows she likes him. 'Otherwise you're wasting your time.'

Privately, traveller girls tell us that, using her sexual magnetism, a girl will make sure that a boy knows she likes him. Some admit they engineer the grab as a way of getting to know the boy better, without the fear of losing their good name. How else can a pair of fifteen-year-olds get to know each other and share a kiss?

As ever, dressmaker Thelma Madine offers a telling insight into just how collaborative the act of grabbing might be. She says, 'Some of the outfits we make are for anyone going to the wedding who hasn't got a fella. They have a "grabbing outfit", but we're not allowed to talk about "grabbing outfits" in front of their parents. The girls will bring you to one side and say, "I want a grabbing outfit." That basically means that they want to find a husband; they're not just looking for a boyfriend, because any boyfriend has to next be the husband. And they probably know who they want that husband to be. We do say if they wear our outfits to a wedding, their chances of getting grabbed are guaranteed!'

CHAPTER FIVE

Rules of Engagement

'Please don't run away with my daughter.
I give consent.'

When a traveller or gypsy couple decides to get married, one final obstacle stands in their way: the girl's father. The couple can't marry unless her daddy says so. After all, Daddy foots the hefty wedding bill.

If the father deems the potential suitor unsuitable, he turns him down. 'No, Mr Wrong, you can't marry my daughter. Goodbye.' Of course, he knows the risk he's taking. The couple might run away. If that happens, then his daughter's name – the family name – is scandalised for ever within their community. In many cases, a run-away is never again reconciled with her family. Their humiliated dad considers them dead. Their name's never mentioned again.

However, even if Mr Right calls to ask for his daughter's hand, the traveller dad's worries are far from over. The race is then on to get his daughter's perma-tanned young pins up the aisle as quickly as possible. Many traveller weddings take place just weeks or months after the couple gets engaged.

The reason for such haste is straightforward – the sooner you book the wedding, the less time there is for the loved-up teenagers to jump the gun. For traveller fathers, their daughter's good name is all. When they discover that she is head over heels in love with a boy, the stakes can't be higher. Here's a girl who's been protected all her life suddenly awakening to alien desires. Here's a girl without worldly wiles under the spell of a sexually repressed young man. Traveller dads are universally terrified that their precious girls will fall at the last hurdle and surrender to their fiancé's desires pre-marriage.

Ex-bareknuckle fighter Paddy Doherty sums up the conflicting emotions of a dad in this situation. 'It's everything, 'cos you've saved your daughter's name. It's enough of a responsibility when someone asks you for your daughter, 'cos all you're afraid of is, "Please don't run away with my daughter now. I give consent. I'll have you married in six weeks or three months," and still like this cocky c*** – excuse my language – is all, "I want your daughter," and he'll run away with your daughter, and you've got to kiss him and keep him sweet, just to get a ring. 'Cos once he's run away with your daughter, he's took her name.'

Thelma Madine has been intimately involved in hundreds of traveller weddings. She explains their 'shotgun' approach to booking the big day: 'Once the Irish traveller girl is asked for, they are married within a couple of months – a couple of weeks sometimes – because they don't want any stigma. One of the things the girls sometimes do, so unpredictable, is run off with a boy. Once they've done that, and spent a night with them, that's it really. They get married and that's it.

'But sometimes the boy brings the girl back and drops her off with the family, and once that girl has been with a guy, the whole community knows about it. She doesn't get married because she's not a virgin and she gets treated bad. Nothing happens to the boy. It is the girl that will go through it then. She might never, ever get asked out again.'

She will rot on the traveller shelf, or hook up with a man deemed 'no good' by the community at large – a gorme – or marry a country man from the settled community. For a traveller dad, having your scandalised daughter shack up with a country man is the ultimate humiliation. You have failed in your number-one duty: to bring up your girl in the traveller way. You have failed to do your bit to preserve the traveller community. Many generations-old traveller feuds have, at their core, a scandalised girl.

So, a traveller dad's most testing day can be the one on which he's asked for his daughter's hand in marriage. First, he has to decide whether or not to sanction the marriage. Is this Mr Right? Even Mr He'll Do? All he has to go on normally is the suitor's family. What is their worth, moral and financial? How do they treat their women? Information is power. If Daddy knows the family and likes their values, it's easy to see how this decision becomes so much more straightforward.

If Daddy says yes, he then has to ensure she remains pure as the driven snow until the wedding day itself. No injury-time own goals. No falling at the last. The scandal monitor is on red alert. The scrutiny is cranked up, her security beefed up. Give them everything they ask for! Chaperone them everywhere! Is it any wonder some couples run away together?

If a traveller dad makes it up the aisle with his daughter unscathed, there is no prouder man. He's giving his daughter away, in church, ideally to a man from a family he respects. That is job done. Mission accomplished. Home and hosed. She's someone else's headache now.

'If the family doesn't allow it, some girls . . . run away. But I never, ever would do that. There'd be me and him but no family. What good is he to you without your family?'

The importance of knowing your potential son-in-law's family proves a major factor in one of *BFGW*'s most unorthodox proposals. The father of seventeen-year-old Priscilla is asked for her hand over the telephone, by a man in a different country. The prospective husband admits that he knows Priscilla mostly from DVDs he's studied of family events. So what does Daddy do?

Priscilla has lived her life in a smart private housing estate in the town of Armagh, Northern Ireland. She's got long, thick, dark brown hair, soft grey-green eyes and an open, innocent baby face. She seems a little bashful and self-conscious. This could be down to the bullying she endured at school, which forced her to quit at fourteen, against her wishes.

'I look the same as them, I dress the same as them – I don't know how they knew I was a traveller,' she says, 'but they did and the names I got called, I couldn't even repeat them. I hated school, but I would have stuck it and done hair and beauty if it wasn't for the bullying.'

Priscilla's voice is soft, sweet with the faintest rural Irish lilt. She dresses conservatively in jeans and hoodies. She's right: you'd never know she's a traveller. Not that she hides it.

Priscilla got engaged at fifteen to Terrance, a boy she barely knew. It was all thanks to that phone call he made to her daddy. Clearly, Daddy approves of the boy's family.

'I knew who he was, and I knew who his family was,' Priscilla says, 'but I didn't know him in the way I know him now. We met more or less at a blessing – you know, the blessing of a grave, like when somebody's a year dead and they put up the headstone and take photos and stuff like that. Loads of people came. Then he seen me in videotapes from other occasions like weddings, 'cos we're in two different countries. Like, he's in London. I didn't have an idea at all that he liked me.'

The first Priscilla knew of Terrance's intentions came from her dad. Terrance had phoned him to ask for Priscilla. Her dad insisted he come to their home in Armagh and ask face to face.

'And then he come to the house and ask again! To see if he'd get a yes or a no from dad first.'

Dad said yes, but Priscilla insists theirs is not an arranged marriage. 'It's not a set-up; it's not like a set-up marriage,' she insists. 'I get to say who I want. I get to say yes and I get to say no. It's up to me, but it's up to dad too.'

Priscilla admits that, had her dad turned down Terrance's request, she would have gone along with his decision. 'If that was the case, I'd have to forget about him,' she says. 'If the family doesn't allow it, some girls take off. They run away with their partner when they're not married, but that's not right. They take off with him, but I never, ever would do that. It would be the worst of the worst; my family would disown me. There'd be me and him but no family. What good is he to you without your family? Your family is the main thing.'

Priscilla observes her family's brand of Irish traveller tradition to the letter. She says, 'My beliefs are the same as any traveller really. Not going out, not going clubbing, not allowed to no discos. I'm allowed to weddings when mum is going and dad's going. We'll go to fairs like Appleby and Stow. I clean the house and cook, and I'll do the same for Terrance.'

She never goes out alone with her fiancé, preferring instead to bring mum along. 'Mum's always there. I don't know . . . I feel comfortable when mum is there.'

When asked if mum's presence deters Terrance from making any sort of sexual advance, it's Priscilla who pounces. 'No, he never would! I'd kill him! He never, ever would.'

Terrance and Priscilla have been, in her words, 'very, very well behaved'.

'You've got to be a virgin on your wedding day. If not, oooh, very bad. Very, very bad. To me anyway . . . to me.'

What would her community's reaction be to news that she wasn't a virgin?

'With us, my family . . . Oh Jesus! Bad. Very bad. Very, very bad. That could be the worst thing that could happen. I really don't know what would happen to me. I haven't got any experience of that, thank God.'

Like a lot of young travellers interviewed for *BFGW*, she is mortified even talking about sex. Refusing to discuss whether or not Terrance is a virgin, she simply says 'He better be!' as she puts it, 'or Mum will kill me stone dead.'

> 'You might move to the other end of the country to cut him out of the pipeline.'

A few generations back, travellers and gypsies arranged their marriages. This doesn't happen any more, of course, but parents do sometimes nudge their sons and daughters in the direction of someone they consider a good catch. Some traveller and gypsy mums and dads start work on Project Perfect Partner the day their child is born.

Helen Collins is an Irish traveller from Manchester with three kids under ten. She explains how some travel-ler mums have been busy sizing up her seven-year-old daughter, Katie. 'I think as babies into little children and then into teenagers, there are always cousins that sort of say, "She could be a potential daughter-in-law." She is keeping her eye on her. You know, for future reference. Maybe for her son. They would even just say, "What about your one and my one?" Then it is just up to you to say yes or no. It is still down to the kids. I would never let her marry anyone she was not happy with. Travellers encourage their child to get to know children they consider a good catch.'

Noreen McDonagh, fifteen, the vivacious cake-shop worker from North Wales, confirms that traveller boys and girls are sometimes deftly coerced into 'the right relation-ship'. 'There's no doubt some travellers these days are married to their cousins because the mother and father of the daughter wanted it,' she says. 'I mean, they're not forced into it – they actually do love each other – but their rela-tionship has been, like, encouraged from a young age.'

When Romany gypsy Thomas asked for fellow Romany Clara Taylor's hand in marriage, her dad, John, was delighted to say yes. 'We know him and we know his family well and we know what they stand for. I couldn't have been happier when he asked.'

Clara, a Jackie O lookalike, agrees. 'You don't just look at the boy; you look at his family. Say there was a man that came home every night and slapped his wife, you're not going to go to his son and marry him. You're going to look for a man that is good to his wife. Good, sensible people.'

What if your daughter is determined to marry a man you're convinced is Mr Wrong? we ask caravan dealer John. He is an easy-going, tolerant and worldly man, yet he says he'd give up business, home, friends, life – everything – to stop it. 'You would leave the country if you had to. You might move to the other end of the country to cut him out of the pipeline. It is a very old-fashioned thing, but we would do it.'

Luckily for John, his daughter is a traditionalist. Clara believes like should marry like, which is why she's alarmed by the growth in mixed-race marriages between gypsies and travellers. 'Me personally, I think it is better if English travellers marry English travellers. Gypsies marry gypsies. I think each kind should stick to their own. I think it would be an easier life if you married your own kind of breed. You would get on better, I think. You would have more of the same ways.

'Like, I think if I married an Irish traveller, we would have a lot of different ways. Maybe our families would have brought us up differently. I don't mean there is anything wrong with them, but it is a completely different way of life. I think you should marry your own kind.'

John is more liberal than his daughter about marriages between different ethnic traveller groups. However, what he insists can't work is a marriage between a traveller and a gorger. 'A fish and a bird couldn't be married, because one wants to live in the sea and one wants to live in the sky. That is what we believe. If a non-traveller girl married my son now, she wouldn't be happy going around in a gypsy caravan. If he was in a house with no other gypsies to socialise with, he'd say, "I feel awful."

'The reason why we like to stick to our own people is because the couple then has got the same upbringing. They will probably get on really well together and then bring up the children the same. Whereas if they've got a different culture, it can cause clashes. It causes problems with the children.'

'Since I have met Sam, I have had better things to do. I don't drink much any more, maybe once a week. I don't gamble any more. She has made me a better person.'

English gypsy Pat Skye Lee, twenty, is breaking centuries of tradition by marrying a non-gypsy. The tree surgeon from St Helen's is marrying a gorger girl he's known since childhood, seventeen-year-old barmaid Sam Norton.

Pat reveals that Sam has already had a positive influence on his life. 'Before I got with Sam, I was quite a shy person. I used to drink a lot as well, which I am not very proud of, and gamble. I had a problem with gambling. Since I have met Sam, I have had better things to do. I don't drink much any more, maybe once a week. I don't gamble any more. She has made me a better person.'

Sam is a shapely brunette with dark skin and big brown eyes. She has always been a rebel: brassy, up for a scrap, with a touchpaper temper. As a kid, she was the only one of her gang who dared walk into Pat's trailer site and ask him out to play.

They lost touch in their early teens. Then, two years ago, a fateful meeting in the street saw Pat ask Sam out. Their friendship rebooted, romance blossomed. On New Year's Eve, Pat proposed. They marry in ten weeks.

Sam reveals the reaction of her settled friends to the news. 'I think most of my friends are, like, shocked because I'm getting married so young, like, at seventeen, but on

Facebook and that everybody is saying, like, "She's getting married to a traveller!"'

'People think they're monsters, don't they? When, like, me and Pat was arguing ages ago, all my friends were like, "You've just had a big argument with a gypsy." I said, "No, I just had an argument with my boyfriend." I said, "Have you never had a row with your boyfriend?" And she said, "Yeah," and I went, "Well, he's my boyfriend. He's not any different."'

Sam is frequently mistaken for a traveller. There's no obvious reason why this should happen. She wears lots of make-up, big spangling jewellery and vivid colours, and often plaits or scrapes her hair back, but then so do lots of girls. Maybe it's the mindset she's adopted since dating Pat.

Pat reveals, 'When she says that she is not a traveller, they are like, "You're lying. You're definitely a traveller." I have definitely put the traveller stamp on her.'

Pat is preparing her for life as a gypsy wife, an outsider. 'She'll be victimised for it, like, treated differently. I have told her what could potentially happen and she's OK with it. She knows what she is facing. We love each other. Whatever else, we are ready for that.'

Sam first samples gorger racism when she tries to book a bigger venue for their reception. 'I had already gone in and booked it,' she says. 'As soon as Pat come in to have a look at the venue, the manager then decided not to let us have it. She told us straight out, "You're not having it because he's a gypsy."'

Resistance to their engagement has also come from within the gypsy community. 'Everyone was like, "Oh, what you going out with a non-traveller girl for? Why you doing that?"' says Pat. 'And I'm like, "Well, it's my choice. It's my life. I can do what I want." There will be some travellers thinking, Well, I don't know how he could possibly do that – marry someone from the non-travelling community. It's not done. I want to show people at home that yes, it can be done. Why not?'

A few days later, Sam gets a taste of gypsy racism. She and her numerous bridesmaids – a mixture of gypsy and non-gypsies – have gathered for a corset fitting when all hell breaks out.

The chat turns to gypsy and non-gypsy cultural differences. Pat's cousin Elycia declares that 'Gorgers say things that they shouldn't say.'

Sam agrees. 'Certain swear words and things that they come out with, I agree that's not appropriate.'

With Sam's settled friends looking on, Elycia cranks up the hostility. 'For instance, we'd die before we'd swear in front of a man. Or I wouldn't even swear in front of me mum, but a gorger person just out – plonk – says it and it's shameful. They've got no respect for whoever's around them or nothing.'

Sam launches a gorger grenade. 'Kiss my arse, Elycia,' she shouts. 'Kiss me arse. I'm just shameful and come out with anything.'

As Pat looks on bemused, Elycia tries to calm her. 'Yeah, but you know, how long have you been in the family? You know what to say and what not to say.'

'Ssh, now,' says Sam, her big eyes ablaze. 'You're making me upset talking about my . . . my culture, and it's not nice.'

After a frosty silence, Sam calms down enough to offer a more measured assessment. 'The only people that judges me is the travellers that don't know me thinking, Ah, what's he marrying her for? They're the only people that judge me, but I don't care what they think, because, at the end of the day, I love him and he loves me, and we're not marrying them – we're marrying each other.'

However, a woman from the settled community doesn't just marry a gypsy; she marries into a rich and complex culture with its own unique values, rules and customs. Sam has found herself flummoxed a few times already. For example, even though she's engaged to Pat, Sam is not allowed to stay over on his site, even in a friend's trailer.

'His sister used to ask me did I want to stay on the same site,' Sam reveals. 'It was, like, five or six plots down. His dad wouldn't let me.'

They don't kiss in public or show any signs of affection in front of his family.

'If he's going out, he won't give me a kiss goodbye or nothing like that. It's just a respect thing. We don't kiss in front of anyone basically! It's not a done thing,' Sam explains. 'In front of his parents he won't sit next to me. At dos it's, like, women one side, fellas the other. I kicked off at him the first time because I wanted him to sit next to me. He said, "Well, I can't exactly sit with you and all the women, can I?"'

To Sam's surprise, the gender divide isn't just public. It's right at the heart of gypsy life. 'So, like, they don't believe that a man should even be in the kitchen. I don't know why. So, like, men won't get up and make themselves a sandwich. They say, "Mum, make me a sandwich."

They won't even get up and make themselves a cup of tea, or make one for a guest.'

There are bigger culture shocks to come. After their wedding, the newlyweds move into a trailer on Pat's site.

'There's no showers, no baths, nothing,' says Sam. 'No amenities. You have to boil a kettle for hot water. I'd be going home every day for a shower. It's only round the corner.'

Sam's worried about noise. The compact Earlestown Traveller site is right next to a busy railway line. 'The trains are going past all the time. I won't be able to sleep,' she says. 'It's dead loud. Nobody who lives on the site thinks it's loud, but I think it's really loud, me. Pat says I better get used to it. He says sites are always hidden behind a railway or behind a McDonald's.'

Sam's been a regular on the site for two years. Everything else about it appeals to her, especially Pat's family.

'They're proper, proper clean,' she says. 'I've never known anybody so clean in my life. Like, people say that they're scum, but they're nothing like that. They are the nicest people you'd ever meet, I think. I feel proud that I'm marrying into them because not many people do and I'm really glad that they have accepted me and that they have let me in.'

In true traveller style, Sam wants eight kids and then to spend the rest of her young life as a stay-at-home mum. However, dressmaker Thelma Madine foresees problems for Pat and Sam, especially when kids arrive and points out just how rare it is for a traveller to marry a non-traveller. She's dressed hundreds of weddings and can recall just three involving a gorger bride or groom. None of them was a gypsy wedding.

'Like, his immediate family might accept her,' says Thelma, 'but that family goes on and on and other people might not accept her. It might become too much for her to try and break into it. We think that racism goes one way. It also goes the other way. Some of the travellers will look down on her for being a non-traveller.'

Thelma explains why children may prove the flashpoint. 'She'll have different ideas about bringing the children up to the way traveller girls bring their children up. They'll clash on issues like schooling for sure.'

A woman who made the same move – from settled community to a traveller site – cautions Sam that she faces far more hurdles to happiness than all-night trains and a lack of hot water. Angela asks not to be identified for fear of making her current situation worse.

'I think the toughest thing for Sam is that everyone's going to know her business,' she warns. 'There's no privacy on a site whatsoever. You do anything and they are going to know within two minutes. The trailers are never locked. They go in and out of one another's caravans without knocking, so, you know, basically your life's an open book – anyone can come in and read it.'

Angela says Pat may decide to take to the road at any time. She wonders how well Sam will cope in a trailer when she hasn't got her parents and their central heating just around the corner. 'In the travelling community, it is the man who decides where the family lives,' she explains. 'He has to go where the work is and she has to go along with it. They'll be no hot showers then. She might find herself having to wash with cold water in the sink of a disabled toilet at a service station. See how romantic she finds trailer life then.'

> 'In the travelling community, it is the man who decides where the family lives. He has to go where the work is and she has to go along with it.'

Josie McFadden started going out with Swanley Smith four months ago. Their wedding is now fast approaching. In a one-to-one interview, Josie is asked how many boyfriends she had before Swanley.

'I am not answering that question. I am not talking about that. No! Don't bring boyfriends into it. Don't bring that word, that B-word. I am not saying that I had another boyfriend.'

To outside observers, it looks like many traveller girls marry their very first boyfriend.

'It is not like only one boyfriend and that boyfriend you have to marry,' she explains. 'It does happen – don't get me wrong. Some girls meet one person and actually fall in love together and marry that person. Their first boyfriend, kind of thing.'

However, Josie says it doesn't matter how many exes a traveller girl has had, since all she has done is kiss them. 'It is just a kiss at the end of the day. That is it. A kiss doesn't mean that you are in love. Travelling girls can have other boyfriends. When you know you love him, and he knows he loves you, and you want to get married, then you go for it.'

By settled society's norms, Josie's journey from single-dom to marriage in less than a year is lightning fast. However, Josie points out the perils of a long-term relationship for a traveller girl. If it doesn't end in marriage, then rumours will circulate that the girl is, as she puts it, 'a wrong 'un'.

'The rumours go around, not very nice ones. Most girls don't like staying with a boy that long. Especially if they love him and he says he loves her. Why hasn't he said, "Let's get married. I am going to go in and ask if I can marry you"? That is the way it works. So a couple of months is not too bad. A year is not too bad. But anything over a year and I would end it.'

Swanley and Josie say their relationship is pretty typical of young traveller couples. Their first date was at a cinema in Watford, to see *The Princess and the Frog*. Disney set the tone for the fairy-tale romance that followed.

'Roughly after about two weeks, I knew I loved her,' reveals Swanley. 'Never wanted to. You know, she's a bit young. Then, when I had gone out with her for four weeks, I just had no choice, I suppose. I thought, You can't stop this. I just looked at her and thought, Yeah, this is the woman I am going to marry. That was it. She is the one.'

'I just knew that he was the one,' swoons Josie. 'It is a feeling, like. You can't explain love, can you? I don't know how, but I just knew after about a week tops. I knew the first few days, but I knew for sure after a week.'

Nineteen-year-old Swanley feared one issue would thwart their romance – her tender age of sixteen. Fitting, then, that Josie's childlike qualities are the very thing he loves most. 'She is different,' he says. 'She is childish but fun childish. Cute, as you say. Most girls are stuck up.'

Within a matter of just three weeks, Swanley began to hint at marriage. They got engaged a week before Easter – six weeks after their first date. However, for Swanley, convincing Josie to say yes was the easy part.

'You know, before you actually ask a girl to wed, you have got to ask the dad first,' he says. 'We were at the pictures. What did we watch? *Kick-Ass*, fittingly enough. And I was telling her, "I want to come back and ask for you."'

Josie takes up the story. 'I was sitting there, but I couldn't breathe. I was in another world, all butterflies.'

Swanley realised it was the moment of truth. 'So there was nothing for it: I had to come back and ask Big Chris.'

Big Chris McFadden is dad to Josie and her eight younger siblings. He's a non-traveller and married Irish traveller Josie Senior eighteen years ago. Since then, he has adopted many traveller ways. But Swanley foresaw several reasons why Big Chris McFadden might have said a big fat McNo: Josie was just sixteen; they'd been going out for only six weeks; Swanley is an English traveller, the McFaddens Irish; the two families didn't know each other well; and Swanley and Big Chris barely knew each other at all.

Swanley and Josie describe the big moment.

Recalls Swanley, 'Josie went into the kitchen to make tea. I got up to sit next to him. As I stood up, I said, "Chris, what it is . . ." and I can't stop now because I have already started. I didn't want to say it standing up. I wanted to say it sitting down right next to him. That way, he hasn't got that far to swing. You know what I mean? There's pillows and children's blankets and things next to Chris, so I'm trying to move the stuff out the way as quickly as I can so I can ask the question. Safe to say, I was a little nervous.'

Josie picks up, 'I was hiding at the door of the kitchen, listening in, pretending to make tea. I was excited, but I don't know . . . I was a bit nervous as well. So it was a weird feeling. I hear Swanley say, "Chris, I have got something to ask you." Daddy thought it was about work or something and he said, "Yeah, what is it?" and then he said, "Can I marry your daughter?" and Daddy's face dropped.'

Josie reveals that Chris didn't say anything for what seemed like several minutes. Then he called his wife down from upstairs.

Josie recalls every second. 'And he goes, "The man wants to marry my daughter. The man wants to marry my child. I am tongue-tied. What am I supposed to say to the man?" They call me out of the kitchen and then Daddy said, "Do you want to marry Swanley?" and I said, "Yes, Daddy," and then, "Are you sure this is what you both want?" Me and Swanley said, "Yeah," and then he went, "Well, you are getting married, then. That is it, then – my baby girl has gone." My Daddy just don't look like my Daddy. I cried because my Daddy's face, he just dropped his face. He wasn't crying, but his eyes filled up and Mummy started crying and then I started crying.'

Chris has very straightforward marriage advice for his spirited and strong-willed eldest girl. 'My advice to Josie is just do as her husband asks her and to be – what is the word? – subservient to her husband, because obviously he

has got to take the lead, him being the man. Then everything should run smooth.'

At sixteen, Josie believes she's ready for marriage. 'Well,
I won't be sixteen when I get married; I will be seventeen,'
she points out. 'Seventeen is a very normal age to get
married. My mummy was seventeen when she got married.
So it is not a big deal when you are seventeen, but sixteen,
I think myself, is a bit young, but I am only engaged now,
aren't I?'

Engagement doesn't alter the unwritten rules. Swanley
still has to return to his family's site in Surrey each night.
Whenever the couple go out, they are chaperoned by a
family member. This will continue right up until the
wedding day – an occasion, needless to say, Josie has been
dreaming about since she was in nappies.

'From the time you are a baby, you are saying, "Ooh, I
like that dress. I'm gonna have that on me wedding day."
Now it is actually happening!'

Josie has a unique idea for her wedding dress, which,
she believes, will kick-start a traveller trend. 'There are
going to be copies of my dress,' she says, 'because it is so
nice. Everybody is going to copy it. Nobody has done
this kind of dress before. It is all about the dress, isn't it?
Mine is going to be a bit different. I'm not going to give
it away, just to say mine is going to be a Spanish kind of
theme wedding.'

Once they are married, Swanley and Josie will live in the
traditional traveller way. He will go out and work; she will
stay at home to cook, clean and have babies.

Swanley has no truck with house husbands. 'The man

has got to go to work,' he says. 'There would be something wrong with him if he didn't go to work. If the woman ever went out to earn the money and the guy stayed at home to look after the children, he would be a funny dude! I am telling you. There would definitely be something wrong there. I can't see that ever happening in our community.'

He knows exactly what he wants from a wife, though he's less sure about what she might want from him. 'I am never bored around her,' he says. 'To me, that makes a good wife. She is a good cook. She does clean-up through most of the day; that is a good sign. Those are really the main things. You know, we get on well. Do I think I will be a good husband? It depends on whether she has been a good wife. I will try as hard as I can.'

Part of Swanley's role as breadwinner is to provide a home for his new wife. Originally, they'd planned to live in a trailer with his family in Surrey, but with the axe hanging over that site, Swanley has reluctantly agreed to live in a house near Josie's parents, in West London. But he's laying down the law about the décor.

'I am not allowed to choose any of the colours,' says Josie, 'because if it was me, then I would do the house up as a Barbie house. All pink.'

'I am letting her have one shocking-pink plasma TV and one shocking-pink DVD player,' says six-foot-five Swanley. 'Both of them is staying in the bedroom. So that is it. That is the only shocking pink.'

'You said that I could have the bathroom pink,' says Josie.

'OK, you can do the bathroom in shocking pink,' he says.

Josie admits that she struggles to get excited about the

house – or anything else beyond her wedding day. 'I have got bigger things on my mind right now,' she squeals.

'I am not allowed to choose any of the colours,' says Josie, 'because if it was me, then I would do the house up as a Barbie house. All pink.'

An uncharitable commentator said some of the *BFGW* girls look like they put their make-up on in the dark. At a traveller site on the outskirts of Trowbridge, in rural Wiltshire, two girls are doing just that. Getting ready for a night out while squeezed in a caravan with a faulty generator is second nature to these girls. They are best friends, nineteen-year-old Irish travellers Bridget Ward and Elizabeth Doran.

In truth, neither girl needs to trowel on so much slap. They are both stunners. Bridget is slim, blonde and blue-eyed with delicate features. She's quietly spoken, thoughtful, a bit of a worrier. Elizabeth, with her long, black hair and green eyes, is noisy proof that opposites attract. She's a bundle of energy, inquisitive, headstrong and loyal – definitely the boss.

But not tonight. It's Bridget's hen night. To mark the occasion, the girls are donning outlandish outfits and lashings of slap. Swindon won't know what's hit it.

In a week's time, Bridget marries Patrick, whom she met at her cousin's wedding in London. He is her second boyfriend.

In her disarmingly thick and throaty traveller twang,

Bridget describes how they first got together. 'He was going with someone else at the time I seen him. I didn't want to dance with him at first, and then he dragged me up. "Oh come on, dance with me," and all things like that and we started dancing and that was it. Then I never heard from him. I heard that he was trying to get me number for to ring me and, erm, yeah, that was it.'

Patrick gave her a real ring just three months later, when he proposed on Christmas Day. In breakneck traveller fashion, they planned to marry in March – taking Bridget from wedding wallflower to blushing bride in six months flat. Needless to say, best friend Elizabeth landed the job of best woman.

That was nearly twelve months ago. The wedding never took place.

That same spring, Elizabeth's dad, Larry, died suddenly. She is still heartbroken. Needless to say, she withdrew as Bridget's best woman.

Bridget and Elizabeth have grown up together, planning their wedding days in tandem, so for one to marry without the other present was unthinkable. Consequently, Bridget postponed the wedding for twelve months. Friends? Unshakeable.

'We used to think about getting married all the time,' laughs Bridget, 'but we didn't think what kind of man we wanted. That never come to me head. I wanted to have me own car, me own Bentley. Black outside and pink leather inside. A really classy dress. Me own home and things like that. That's what we thought about.'

In a week's time, Bridget's going to have to do without the Bentley, but, thanks to Daddy and Paddy, all her other wedding fantasies are coming true. First, though, she must give single life a good send-off. The girls' outfits might be wild, but their night out won't be! They don't drink, smoke or talk to country boys. Plus bride-to-be Bridget still lives under Daddy's benign but unbending rule. This hen night has a 10 p.m. curfew.

Traveller marriages also come with a set of strict rules, which is why this night is such a milestone in Bridget and Elizabeth's lifelong friendship.

Elizabeth explains, 'Yeah, I'm happy in one way, for Bridget, but sad because this is the last time that I'm ever going to go out with her. Like, when she's married, she's not going to be able to do this. Once she's married, she can't go out just with her friends. She can't go anywhere without her husband. I just hope she has a really good time because this is the last time she and I can do this.'

The marriage of Bridget and Patrick marks the estrangement of Bridget and Elizabeth in another way: the newlyweds are moving to London.

'On the wedding day, it's going to be very emotional,' says Elizabeth privately, 'but as long as she's happy, it's the main thing. I don't know, I just hope ... I hope she don't change herself. That, like, us being friends and things, I just hope that don't change.'

Finally the girls are ready. Bridget wears a perilously short pink dress, a white wedding veil, a sash, a white feather boa, a pink feather in her hair and an industrially robust layer of make-up. On her exposed upper thigh flashes a comedy garter. Her best woman is similarly pink and burlesque. When Bridget's younger brother Larry comes to the caravan door and clocks their saucy costumes, he throws a fit.

'You're a holy show! What in the name of God are you wearing?' he asks in disbelief. When he sees the garter on Bridget's leg, he loses it altogether. 'Take it off now. Take that off your leg now!'

The girls ignore Larry and jump giggling into a waiting taxi. At least this car has turned up. Days earlier, Elizabeth ordered a pink limo for the hen night. When it failed to show up on time tonight, she rang the hire company. The nice man on the phone explained that they don't go out to traveller sites.

'Sixteen year old and drinking. She's only married two months and she's drinking!'

For one night only, Surrey's own Cinderella, Lizzie Lee, swapped the mop for a microphone at her karaoke hen night. The next day, little sis Susie, sixteen, had to face the music – when Daddy learned she'd misbehaved.

Sadly for Susie, in one photo she forgot to put her drink down – out of frame, out of sight. When her dad saw the snap of boozy Susie this morning, he flipped.

Lizzie explains what happened next. 'He says, "My child's drinking." He's rung her, telling her off. "Sixteen year old and drinking!" I said, "But, Daddy, she's married two months." "Exactly – she's only married two months and she's drinking!"'

'We walked out the doors and they'd blocked the whole street with police.'

Violet Anne Stubley is the twenty-two-year-old Romany gypsy from the idyllic village of Stanton-under-Bardon in Leicestershire. She's the *Good Health* cover girl with glowing skin, shiny hair and a no-nonsense approach to life. In a few weeks' time, the hotel receptionist hosts a reception of her own when she marries Larry, a twenty-one-year-old Romany who doesn't want to be identified for the usual reasons.

The pair met three years ago at the Stow-on-the-Wold Horse Fair. The day after they marry, they move to a traveller site in Slough, Berkshire, next to Larry's parents.

Violet Anne has finished planning almost every element of her epic nuptials. Last week, she adjusted her sights to her hen night.

She says, 'Friday night was going to be the hen night. We was going to have a girls' night out, in a pub, club or something, and literally put a bit of food on. That's what me mother wanted me to do.'

However, when venues learn that Violet Anne is a gypsy, they turn down the booking.

'Because we're gypsies, everything's getting cancelled. Everywhere we go to, we put down a booking and it's OK, but then we go down there to confirm and get down to the arrangements and it's like, "You're not booked." They deny we booked it and we have to turn round and leave.'

Violet Anne has explained to venue managers that the evening is testosterone-free; just young women having a drink and a dance. That holds no sway with the licensed landlords of Stanton-under-Bardon. So, out of desperation, they try a rough old dive in a town some miles away, but they too cancel.

'It's really, really bad,' says Violet Anne. 'It was disgusting. For her to send a text to wheedle her way out of it saying they can't let us have this function room, it just torments you. They think we're not good enough for the county's worst doss-hole? It's just horrible, really. It just aggravates you when you just want a normal good time and then you see these drug addicts, these drug dealers, going down there doing their business. They allow all that, but they won't allow young girls just to have a night out.'

Violet Anne has given up. 'It's just too much hassle. I've just put a stop to it. If the girls come and get me out, then that's fine, but I've not got anything organised. I'm sick of it.'

A few days later, determined that Cinderella shall have her hen night, Violet Anne's gang find a venue where they're welcomed with open arms.

'When we got into the bar, they said it was open till four o'clock in the morning and we could have food in there and I don't know what else,' Violet Anne explains.

The girls dance, chat, drink, laugh, invite the locals to join in . . . then everything changes.

Violet Anne is still none the wiser. 'At ten o'clock, they told us to get out, there was too many gypsies, and we had to get out. We walked out the doors and they'd blocked the whole street with police and we had to come home. We had no choice of it. Too many gypsies – you'll have to leave. It was like somebody had done a murder. There was no trouble at all.'

The next day, Violet Anne returned to the bar to retrieve a friend's forgotten handbag.

'I said to them, "Look, we wasn't going to murder you. All we wanted to do was fill your till and have a good time." I said, "Why did you say you was closing at four in the morning and kick us out at ten?" He said, "I never said that." He promised us everything. He promised us the world. Some people had come from miles away and had to leave ten minutes after arriving.'

Violet Anne worries that her wedding might turn out the same. When the venue finds out that they're gypsies, management might cut the night short, or cancel the reception altogether. Her guests might turn up to a very different reception – a line of policemen charged with sending the unwanted revellers packing. Sadly, Violet Anne is one of several *BFGW* brides terrified that her reception may never happen.

'Some people think of marriage as throwing away your life, but in a traveller's point of view, it is the beginning of your life.'

Cindy McDonagh from Cheshire has no such worries. Cindy's dad – who doesn't want to be identified – is clearly loaded. He's booked a country-house estate in Cheshire for

133

her ceremony and her reception. No racist chain-hotel manager will be cancelling Cinderella McDonagh's do at the last moment.

Cindy is a ringer for *Shrek*'s Princess Fiona – the non-ogre version – though she's a bit shapelier, a brunette and sunbed brown. Cindy is bustling – a little bossy. Think a caring, if slightly overbearing, primary-school teacher.

At twenty-one, Daddy's blue-eyed girl will be an older traveller bride. She reveals her reason for waiting. 'A lot of our friends are married with kids now that never even knew each other. Me and him were going out before they even met, like they have met in the meantime. They have got married and are family people with kids and they never really took the time to get to know each other.'

Cindy is marrying red-haired Irish traveller Johnny. Of course, in Irish-traveller style, Johnny had to man up and ask Cindy's devoted daddy for the hand of his only daughter.

'I think it is the day that a lot of traveller men dread,' says Johnny. 'They just don't look forward to it at all. There are fathers that have said no. It has happened.'

Johnny elected not to seek Cindy's advice.

'No,' says Cindy, 'because I never would have advised him to get drunk first!'

'I don't remember much of it,' Johnny admits. 'I had a few pints down me. I just went blah, blah . . . and blurted it out.'

Whatever he said worked. Cindy is frantically preparing for her wedding, which is going to be a major event, even by traveller standards.

At twenty-one, a lot of country or gorger women would be in higher education or building a career. For Cindy – a capable young woman who could turn her hand to anything – none of that matters. It is all about getting married.

'We don't stay in one place to get an education. We have other priorities. It would be one in a million to find a traveller that is, like, a teacher or lawyer or a doctor.'

Johnny agrees. 'It is not something that we want. It would be very weird to see a traveller with an education.'

Sitting alongside Cindy is another Johnny, her older brother. He too is dark, with intense eyes and an open, friendly face. 'Some people think of marriage as throwing away your life, but in a traveller's point of view, it is the beginning of your life,' he says. 'It is what life is all about. Getting married and settling down and having a family of your own. That is your life, basically. Raise up your family the best way you can, provide and look after them. That is the way it is for the man anyway.'

Johnny accepts that, for any twenty-one-year-old gorger, home life and kids may seem a premature life choice, but he insists that, overall, a travelling life is much more fulfilling than a stationary one.

'You don't just have your settled home; you're not driving down that same road every day,' he says. 'You don't have your nine-to-five job, looking at the same neighbours. You are travelling and meeting different people. It is a better life. We prefer it anyway, and this is why we are so keen on keeping our culture the way that it is.'

Johnny – like many travellers – fears that his human right to roam is being strangled by lawmakers and regulators.

More and more travellers are reluctantly giving up life on the road and settling into homes.

'We are like a dying breed. We are dropping like flies,' he says. 'There is no home for us on the road any more. Laws are always being changed to go against the travelling way of life. We just want people to acknowledge that we play our part in the world and others play their part. Good for them if they want to be lawyers and doctors. They are who they are. We are who we are and this is how we do things.'

CHAPTER SIX

Boy Meets Girl, Old School

'We just went off, pulled a couple of people off the street as witnesses and got married.'

When did blockbuster traveller wedding ceremonies become the norm? Why do travellers stretch to such excess? And how can gypsies or travellers afford twenty-stone dresses, masses of bridesmaids, five-foot cakes, Hummers, Rollers and choppers? One thing is certain: before the 1990s, traveller weddings were nothing like this. Take John Taylor, a Romany gypsy from South Yorkshire. In his day, gypsies and travellers married with as little fanfare as possible.

'I never told my parents that I was getting married to my wife. We just went off, pulled a couple of people off the

137

street as witnesses and got married. We came back and told them the good news afterwards.'

No Bentleys. No bling. Not exactly what our *BFGW* brides have in mind.

> 'I needed a van. I went down to the traveller site to buy a van, bought a van off her mother, seen her daughter and how can I say it? A couple of days after that, I took her on a date and the rest is history.'

Josie's dad, Big Chris McFadden, from West London, has been married to her mum – the original Josie – for eighteen years. Josie Junior is the oldest of their nine kids. Not bad for a couple who knew each other for three days before they got hitched.

Chris explains their whirlwind romance. 'I needed a van. I went down to the traveller site to buy a van, bought a van off her mother, seen her daughter and how can I say it? A couple of days after that, I took her on a date and the rest is history. We decided that we would get married there and then, so I took her away and brought her back with her wedding ring. It was all above board. The papers were there to prove it. There was nothing that anyone could do. That was it.'

Chris is a non-traveller, but you'd never know it. He's adopted their traditions and their ideas – right down to shelling out for showbiz weddings for his daughters. Like most, he can't quite pin down when or why big fat gypsy weddings became the norm. As father of the bride, he knows one thing for sure: the old ways were certainly easier on the wallet.

> 'My own wedding was the first wedding I was ever at in my life.'

One enduring Irish traveller marriage could scarcely have started in less glamorous circumstances. Paddy Doherty, traveller-site caretaker in Salford, near Manchester, and his wife, Roseanne, have been married for thirty-three years. They've had ten kids, though sadly only five survive.

Despite such personal tragedy, Paddy and Roseanne are hilarious, warm and insightful. Here's the inimitable exchange when Paddy first introduces Roseanne to the *BFGW* crew.

Paddy: Roseanne! Woman! This is my wife, Roseanne.

Rosanne: Hello. Pleased to meet you. I'm Roseanne.

Paddy: She's my baby!

Rosanne: I'm his baby!

Paddy: All the way, shum, shum, shum!

Rosanne: OK, don't get carried away.

Paddy: We are Dumb and Dumber! Come on, give me a hug, hug, hug, woman!

[They hug, hard.]

Rosanne: You nearly broke me jaw!

Paddy: I give her whiplash with me chin!

These days, Paddy and Roseanne typify free-spending, cash-rich travellers who enjoy the best of everything. Their pop-video chalet is a showroom of thick pile, marble and Italian designer furniture. Everything in the chalet shines or reflects.

'I think travellers have all got the same taste. It's like the Versace look,' says Roseanne. When asked to describe the Versace look, she struggles. 'It's like the marble effect, um, yeah, the marble effect sort of thing, shiny.'

Paddy has a more succinct definition: 'It's a hole in the pocket.'

Paddy and Roseanne are one of countless rags-to-riches traveller tales. When they got married, in August 1977, their lives could not have been more different. Roseanne wore a borrowed dress, Paddy a cheap suit. Their wedding was second on the bill, latched on late to the main event – the marriage of Paddy's older brother to Roseanne's older sister. In fact, their siblings are the reason for them meeting in the first place.

As Roseanne explains, 'My sister Theresa and his brother Martin was getting married. So when his brother came down to see my sister, she wasn't allowed out unless she had someone with her . . . which was me. So every evening they'd go for a walk. I'd have to stand behind them and walk wherever they walked. And then after about a week and a half, I said to my sister, "I can't do this any more, following yous everywhere. I'm not doing it!" So then Martin went and got his brother Paddy to keep me company as we were walking along after them. And that's how we met!'

Paddy remembers the day he plucked up the courage to ask Roseanne out on a date. 'We were just being polite to each other, weren't we?' he says. 'Walking here and there and keeping her company. One thing led to another and another and then I said, "Do you fancy going to the dance?" And she said, "Yeah."'

Roseanne knew her parents wouldn't let her go. The sixteen-year-old took matters into her own hands. 'Well, Paddy came to the house. I sneaked down to the dance out through the back window. I have a sister called Bridey and she was still in school. I'd only just left school. Bridey wouldn't let me go to the disco unless I brought her, and she was, like, thirteen with her socks up to her knees, so I had to bring her. And she got in with white socks on and everything. I don't know how it happened, but she got in.'

Just as well she did. Romance blossomed that night at the Carousel Dance Hall, although how their first kiss came about, we'll never know. Paddy and Roseanne invest much of their time and energy on banter and ribbing one another. Roseanne insists she can't remember their first kiss – much to Paddy's irritation. Paddy then refuses to say how it came about. Travellers – Irish in particular – tend to be coy about any kind of physical contact with the opposite sex. However, Paddy's happy to reveal how they fell for each other and married just four months later.

'We cared for each other. I don't know, we fell in love with each other. We knew we were meant for each other and that was it. People say how can you know, after four months of going out with a girl? I knew she was the girl I wanted. And she definitely knew I am the man she wanted – know what I mean? There wasn't an "if" or "but" about that!'

Although their four-month courtship is conventional by traveller standards, Paddy's proposal of marriage was anything but. By his own admission, he had no choice in the matter.

'It's funny how me and him got married,' says Roseanne. 'We went out with each other and one day it was about two o'clock in the afternoon and we went off visiting a friend of mine and we got caught in traffic coming back. My mother was back from work at four. We were at the bottom of our street at half past four and I was too frightened to go in because we were not allowed out of the house unless one of the children was with us. Then it came to five o'clock, then it came to six o'clock, then it came to ten o'clock, and I'm only standing at the entrance.'

Because she had failed to get home on time – and then spent so much time alone with a boy – Roseanne had been scandalised. That's why she feared walking through her front door.

'Even looking in through the windows, I can see my mum and dad, but as time went by, I feared them more and more. Then about twelve or one o'clock, mum and dad had gone to bed and we were still sat outside on the street and then we said, "Where shall we go?" Then we went to stay with his aunt Mary and it turned out she wasn't there.'

Next morning, Roseanne and Paddy decided to go home and face her parents' wrath. As they turned into Roseanne's street, the wrath was coming out to meet them.

'We're heading towards our house and who comes out to meet us?' says Roseanne. 'Only me mother and father, and, um, Daddy said to him, "Right, you're going to have to come to the pub with me now." That was as if to say, "You're going to ask for my daughter's hand in marriage." Do you know what I mean? And I'm sat there like Shakin' Stevens thinking, Oh, Daddy, Daddy, Daddy.'

Roseanne's fears were well founded. At that time, her father, also called Paddy, didn't regard Paddy Doherty as a good catch. In fact, he thought Paddy was unhinged.

Roseanne explains his concerns. 'When Paddy's brother Martin used to come down to the house to see Theresa, he'd sit in the living room with my daddy and have a cup of tea and was dead sensible. Paddy would be in the kitchen with us and we'd have the record player. He'd put it on full blast and we'd be dancing and singing in the kitchen and dad would say, "He's mad, that boy. He's mental. He's not sensible like Martin." Daddy was very worried that he was wild.'

Paddy doesn't see it like that at all. 'It was like I was on the fast lane,' he says, 'and my brother Martin was like on the hard shoulder. Very old-fashioned and dressed all nice, and I was doing my own thing. When our Martin was seventeen, it was like he was forty-five. When I was seventeen, I was like fourteen. I was just wild.'

Paddy takes up the story. Roseanne's dad has summoned him to the local pub after their illicit night away. Only Paddy can do justice to what happens next. 'Straight to the pub and at that time I never drunk in my life,' Paddy reveals.

'So he said, "What do you want to drink, son?" I said, "I'll have a glass of Coke." "*What?*" he says. I said, "I'll have a glass of Coke." "Listen," he says, "you're man enough to ask for my daughter, so you're man enough to take a drink off me." Honest to God, that's the way he was. So I say, "I'll just have a glass of Coke." "Did I tell you," he says, "that's my daughter? You'll be man enough to take a drink off me." "'OK, then," I said, "I'll have a half o' Guinness!" He says, "What did I tell you? You're man enough to ask for my daughter, then you're man enough to ask for a pint! 'Cos only a woman drinks a half!"

'He got me this pint and I see this pint and I think, What in the name . . . ? It's gonna give me a heart attack to drink that pint, so it is! I put it to my lips and I just wet it and I put it down and he says, "Listen, son, either you're drinking it," he says, "or you're out that door!" "Oh," I said, "I'll drink it," 'cos I knew then he meant it. You're on your Jack Jones if you don't drink it; you're not having her. I drunk half of it. Oh, I felt a bit dizzy. I said, "I'll go on now, thank you very much." First drink I ever had in my whole life, it was off old Paddy, her old daddy. God rest his soul.'

Four months after they first met, Paddy and Roseanne shared a double wedding with Martin and Theresa. There were no fat dresses, fast cars or fancy cakes.

'I had to get seven children ready that morning,' Roseanne recalls. 'My mother cooked a big fry-up breakfast in the morning. I'm one of nineteen children and nearly everyone was in the house. I did a big breakfast. I had to wash up and then I had to dress, like, six of the youngest and I was ready. I think it was, like, five to eleven or something like that and we were getting married at eleven. No make-up, my hair not even brushed, just rush and gone.

'My dress was very slim, actually, really slim. We borrowed it. Yeah, Theresa's was bought; mine was borrowed. So we had something new, old and borrowed. And then we got something blue to go with it.'

Aged just eighteen and sixteen, Paddy and Roseanne felt overawed by the occasion.

'My own wedding was the first wedding I was ever at in my life until then,' says Roseanne.

'It was a rollercoaster and we didn't know what this was all about,' says Paddy. 'Our Martin fitted in lovely and Theresa fitted in lovely, but me and her were like two fishes out of water. She's looking at me and I'm looking at her. Oh shit! We got problems.'

Even their wedding night proved a calamity.

'On our wedding night,' recalls Roseanne, 'he slept with his father; I slept with his aunt and all her daughters. Turns out we went to the wedding, then we went to Belle Vue, a big disco, and then his father turned up with his sister, and then we went back to his aunt's. We ended up staying there the night in different caravans. Woke up the next morning, like, everything was strange and everybody was strange. I didn't know any of these people. I was like, "I want my mummy. I want my daddy."'

Roseanne's daddy – despite his initial reservations – soon grew to like his wild son-in-law, Paddy Doherty.

'Daddy had a lot of son-in-laws,' says Roseanne, 'and he had something to say about each one. He said, "Paddy's very, very loud, but he's my favourite son-in-law."'

Four of Paddy and Roseanne's five kids are now married. Their wedding days couldn't have contrasted more with that of their parents. These days, traveller and gypsy weddings tend to be major productions – glamorous, exotic and flamboyant, or flashy, overblown and gauche, depending on your tastes.

One thing is beyond dispute: serious money is splurged on these events. Tens of thousands of pounds. Over the next few chapters, *Big Fat Gypsy Weddings* will give you a behind-the-scenes insight into the fattest gypsy weddings on last year's calendar.

> 'It's, like, where did they get the money from? They must have robbed it or done something wrong to get it.'

Why do some traveller and gypsy families stage such extravagant weddings? Some of the *BFGW* brides say it's down to family pride. Weddings have become a status symbol – a statement. No less than the honour of the family name is at stake.

One priest in Lincolnshire has celebrated several traveller occasions. He agrees that pride fuels the excess, but he argues that the statement they are making is aimed at us, not at other travellers.

'Their pride comes out on these occasions,' he says. 'They want to be better than the normal population. They're looked down on as the bottom of the ladder generally in society, but on these occasions, they try to outdo the settler community,

146

to make a statement about who they are, to show they still have pride and have something special. Funerals, weddings, baptisms, they really do the occasions proud.'

Paddy Doherty agrees. 'I'll tell you why travellers want to stand out so much. We've a lot to prove to society, to country people. To be totally honest, a lot of poor travellers can't afford it, but those that can want to show country people that we're just as good as you.'

When did traveller weddings become such brazen spectacles? How much do they cost? And how can travellers afford it?

When travellers get married, one man has to stump up – the father of the bride. As Roseanne Doherty explains, 'We all hope that we only have boys because the girl's family pays for the wedding. The less girls, probably the better.' Paddy and Roseanne hit the jackpot – they have four sons and one daughter, Margaret.

So how much does a big fat gypsy wedding cost? The *Daily Mail* estimates that the average traveller and gypsy wedding costs £140,000. 'That's a lot of tarmac,' reads the spiteful headline. That sets the tone for the rest of the article, which goes on to estimate that the diamond-encrusted wedding dresses cost between £15,000 and £50,000, the cake a grand and the free bar £30,000. Then there's the pimped-up transportation, the squad of bridesmaids, the meals, the honeymoon . . .

'I think that's wildly exaggerated,' says Roseanne.

Like so many issues surrounding the travelling community, what they earn and what they pay is shrouded in secrecy. Travellers and gypsies don't like to talk money.

The people who bring the bling – dressmakers, cake-makers, wedding planners – have been sworn to secrecy. Any revelation would be deemed a breach of confidence. Loose talk costs livelihoods.

Take Thelma Madine, the dressmaker whose multi-layered blancmange creations have, among other novelties, featured mechanical butterflies and LED lights. 'I've known dresses that cost £50,000,' she says, before adding enigmatically, 'I'm not saying that I made them, though.' She refuses to give specifics. 'I would never betray the confidence of anybody, especially the travellers.'

Gill, the boss of ABC Cakes, whose teetering confections defy all conventions, is similarly tight-lipped. 'They cost a lot, obviously,' says Gill, 'but we don't talk about that. It is not all about cost. It is fun for us to do and it is fun to see their faces when it is done, but it is a lot,' she laughs, 'and that is all I am saying on that one!'

It's the same story from wedding planner Gaynor. 'Travellers are very secretive. We don't discuss money whatsoever. That is a big taboo.'

Travellers don't tell each other. The father of the bride won't even tell his wife and daughter how much he's coughed up. As ever with travellers, in the absence of hard facts, myths abound. According to some, travellers propagate these myths. Their daughter's wedding is a status symbol. It is the barometer by which the standing of certain families will be inevitably judged by their peers. So why deny that the flowers cost £65,000, or the dress £50,000? Some travellers think the bigger your wad, the bigger your wallop. Staging a bigger, better, brasher bash than a rival clan is a matter of familial pride.

It is this sense of pride in the family name that helps finance some traveller weddings. Paddy and Roseanne Doherty say it is through family members that much of the wedding wonga is raised. Paddy and Roseanne's clan clubbed together to help finance Margaret's big day. That's a big club: between them, they have twenty-plus siblings.

Paddy explains how it works. 'Say I don't have much money. Well, all my brothers will all donate money, everyone. They don't donate; they lend to you. Like, it's a way of life for the travellers. And they'll all, each one will all give a thousand quid, or a grand and a half per person, so you got a lot. Then all your cousins will find another couple of hundred quid, so you've raised, like, maybe twenty-five, thirty grand, forty grand. I don't have that sort of money.'

Thelma Madine agrees that large and proud extended families are a major source of big fat wedding money. 'The families of the traveller girls will help them all the way along. All their uncles, older brothers will contribute. They all want this extravagance 'cos all their girls' weddings are like a status symbol for their family. They all want her to have the best, to outdo each other.'

The bride's father often has some money put aside too. As soon as a traveller has a daughter, he knows what's coming. Some say they start saving for their daughter's wedding the day she's born.

It's clear that some travellers and gypsies don't need to borrow money from anyone to fund their daughters' fantasy wedding day. They're loaded. It's a fact of life that riles many people in the settled community. The comments on blogs and websites and in newspaper letters pages are as ill informed as they are predictable. 'Where do they get the money for these weddings?' is the number-one FAQ. The replies people post tend to lack any evidential support. They are rich because they don't pay taxes, or because they overcharge people for shoddy work, or because they're criminals. The travelling community acknowledges that a minority is engaged in criminal activity and/or provide shoddy work. Same as in the settled community, they say. But the simple answer is that they pay for the weddings in the same way country people do: by working hard, saving up and making some sacrifices.

Of course, the travellers and gypsies on *Big Fat Gypsy Weddings* don't tell us how much they're worth or how they make their money. When we ask the next best thing – the people that deal with them – they prove evasive. But when we push them, we gain a little insight.

Thelma Madine knows several traveller and gypsy families. She does business with them. It might come as a shock to the commentators above that Thelma's clients don't pay in rolls of grubby notes. They write cheques or transfer money from their high-street bank account to hers.

'People see these big weddings and funerals. It's, like, where did they get the money from? They must have robbed it or done something wrong to get it,' says Thelma. 'In most or maybe all of the travelling families, the men work very hard,' she says. 'They own their own companies. We know one who owns a pony-and-trap company, another a furniture company, and you know they have earned their money the hard way, it hasn't been given to them. They set up these companies because of the children. As soon as their girl is born, they know they are going to have to pay for a wedding and they won't let her down. They will start saving to pay for these weddings.'

What Thelma and other close observers of the community say is that travellers have the same amount of money as average working families. They just use it in different ways.

'Their priorities are different to ours,' Thelma points out. 'We think more about the mortgage. Their priorities, if you talk to them, is about the dress, what they look like – you know that's what's important to them. I mean, I look at them and think, Oh my God, I could have given a deposit for a house rather than buy a dress like that! But that's what they enjoy. In their community, it gives them pride. They are very proud people, very, very proud. They don't like anyone talking about them. They put on a good, good party and they get talked about in a good way. And that's good for the family.'

Most settled people have to contend with a hefty mortgage. The British Banking Association states that the average home loan in the UK is about £150,000. Most travellers and gypsies own their trailers. Many see the settled community as mortgage slaves. Traveller money isn't tied up in bricks and mortar. Many travellers and gypsies value portable and visible wealth. They spend their money on items they can transport easily and that give them kudos in the community: flashy cars, gold jewellery, designer furniture, big fat weddings.

Paddy explains the importance of flash wheels. 'Cars and vans and trucks and caravans are very important to travellers. You're explaining with each vehicle, "I'm not begging off anyone!" Like as long as you got a nice turnout – "turnout" means a nice car, lorry and a trailer – a respectable turnout, then people know you're your own man. You want nicer things than other people's got, so you work harder to get a nicer car, a nicer trailer, a nicer van, whatever it may be.'

'Because our wealth tends to be on show,' says one traveller who owns his own business but doesn't want to be identified, 'you can rest assured that the tax man is taking note and wants to know where it came from. We live under the same laws as everyone else.'

The wonderland weddings of the past fifteen years coincide with a dramatic upturn in the fortunes of some travellers and gypsies. For a start, the value of scrap metal has soared. Most travellers can turn their hands to scrapping – 'We collect their rubbish; everyone's a winner.'

Many people are unaware that the reclamation industry is one of the world's top ten in terms of value. It employs hundreds of thousands of people. In the more industrialised countries, scrap metal accounts for at least 45 per cent of steel production. There are similar scrap ratios for copper, lead, zinc and aluminium. Research in Ireland shows that the major market for scrap metal is Irish Steel. Sixty per cent of Irish Steel's raw material is sourced from scrap collected by travellers. That's 75,000 metric tonnes, with a value of £1.5 million. Of course, this is not the only company that gets scrap from travellers, but it gives an indication of the profits on offer.

Another boost – particularly to mobile Irish travellers

– was the Republic of Ireland's Celtic Tiger economic boom. For almost a decade in Ireland, tradesmen with skills in block-laying, plastering, scaffolding or tarmacking earned thousands of euros a week.

Of course, on the other end of the scale, many travellers struggle. Jobs like jet-washing and tree-topping won't make anyone rich. Some experience genuine hardship. Others earn what they need and are satisfied with that. Almost all the travellers on *BFGW* say that they're better off than ever before.

While bride-to-be Cindy McDonagh splurges her daddy's money on a helicopter, an LED dance floor and two Beckham-esque silver thrones for her big day, her brother Johnny provides a grounded perspective. He warns that newfound wealth isn't enriching these age-old cultures. 'These last twenty years or so, more people has been coming into money. There is an old saying that money is the root of all evil, and I truly believe that. I believe that money has changed an awful lot of people. No one will do nothing for you now. People want to see you with nothing and see themselves with everything. It's all about the "me" rather than the community. It's become sort of like a best thing now. It's about who's got the nicer car and who's wearing the nicer clothes. At big occasions here, you get a lot of eyes. It's very important to put up a good impression. I think that people were more content with the way they were years ago,' he says. 'There was no such thing as best and everyone was equal.'

CHAPTER SEVEN

Dress Rehearsal

'It is all about the dress. Who has got the biggest dress?
As soon as you get back from a wedding it is, "What was
this like?" and, "What was that like?" That is basically
why you do it.'

One thing dominates most traveller girls' thoughts from childhood – their wedding dress. Most of the brides-to-be on *BFGW* happily admit that their wedding dress has been a lifelong obsession – the summit of their young dreams.

Every Cinderella needs a fairy godmother to make her dreams come true. Step forward our friend Thelma Madine. This savvy Liverpudlian dressmaker has turned excessive traveller taste into a lucrative business. Thelma gets travellers. She doesn't look down on them. She doesn't kowtow to them either. She's well able to take care of herself. However, she believes there is one key reason why travellers have embraced her: trust.

'You know, it is hard to break into the traveller community, really hard,' she says. 'They don't let people in, because they don't trust people. Usually people who try and get in there have some ulterior motive. They know that I am not going to tell anybody what they have paid. They know I am not going to tell another family what sort of wedding dress they are having. They trust me. Once they trust you, that is it.'

Perhaps some travellers relate to Thelma because hers too is a rags-to-riches tale. She's enjoyed designing and making dresses since her teens. However, in the 1980s, her hobby turned into her only chance of making a living. A divorce left her broke and in debt with kids to care for. So, Thelma began to sew her way out of debt. She made dresses and sold them from a market stall in Liverpool.

One day, a chance query from a traveller girl at the market changed her life. The girl asked Thelma if she could make dresses 'like the ones in *Gone with the Wind*'. Thelma recalls, 'I said, "Do you mean velvet and sticking out with a bonnet?" and she basically said, "Yeah." She wanted three in red for her little girls, so she said she would be back the following week to pick them up.'

Thelma plunged much of her money and all of her time into making three perfect little *Gone with the Wind* outfits. The following Saturday, she waited and waited . . . The traveller girl never turned up. Thelma was crushed, but then she noticed something.

'There was so much interest in these dresses. All the travellers that were going past were basically saying, "How much are they? How much are they?" and I thought, I've hit on something here.'

Thelma sold those three, and a whole lot more. Then, when a traveller girl asked Thelma to make her wedding dress, her fortunes went cosmic. For four laborious weeks, the fussy bride-to-be kept telling Thelma she wanted it bigger, with more diamonds. Bigger! More diamonds! When that girl finally shuffled awkwardly up the aisle, her big sparkling dress caused a sensation. Word about *that* dress fizzed throughout the traveller community. The orders flooded in. They wanted them bigger, sparklier, longer. Thelma and her sister-in-law stitched and slaved in a draughty garage for a few years until finally, in 1994, she opened Nico. This little shop has produced the biggest fattest gypsy wedding dresses ever made.

These are some of Thelma's most spectacular creations to date. The longest was a dress with a train measuring 217 feet. That's the length of four buses. Crucially for the bride, that train was a couple of feet longer than the one hauled up the aisle by her cousin a few months earlier. 'It had to be rolled up like a scroll,' Thelma recalls.

The most unusual was the swan dress. The bride wanted to look like she was floating inside a swan. Her wedding was in three days' time. Thelma took it on when the girl explained why she wanted a swan dress: 'Because swans stay together for ever.'

The biggest weighed twenty-seven stones. It was for bride Carly O'Brien, who hit the scales some twenty stones lighter. 'There was loads of steel in it,' says Thelma, 'to keep the dress from collapsing and swallowing the little bride. She just couldn't move at all. She was pushed and shoved all day. It must have been killing her.'

One dress proved so ungainly for the bride that her family couldn't even drag her around. Resourceful Thelma found a solution. 'She just could not walk in the dress, so we got the trainers what the kids have with the wheels in. She had to be pushed down the aisle because there was no way she could have walked.'

Thelma and her team can't always make the bride's fairy-tale fantasy come true. One wanted her entire wedding dress covered in Swarovski crystals. 'This would have meant millions, not thousands, of crystals on her dress. She just wouldn't have been able to stand up in it for the weight, never mind anything else, so we had to put her off that. She just had her top covered in Swarovski, like Jordan did.'

The designer visions of two other brides were thwarted by copyright law. One wanted the Chanel interlocking 'C's logo sewn into her dress, the other 'D&G', as in Dolce & Gabbana. In Swarovski crystals, of course.

Where does this need for traveller brides to stand out come from? Why do so many traveller girls crave fairy-tale wedding dresses? Thelma believes it is instilled in them from birth. 'Little girls love the whole romantic thing in fairy-tales. Traveller girls know they can actually get to live that fairy-tale. That's gonna be their day. *The* day of their lives. No matter what comes along, nothing will touch that day. Even now, we speak to girls we've done, like, ten years ago and they say that they still think about their wedding every day.'

Most fairy-tale weddings have Disney themes, with the latest movie sparking a copycat scramble. 'With *The Princess and the Frog* just coming out, we have had a lot of girls asking for that dress,' says Thelma. 'We have actually just done one and it is really amazing. She has got a little brother dressed as the prince as well. It will be exciting to see that wedding.

'I think we got six requests for the *Coming to America* dress with the big long train on it, the pink one.'

These twenty-stone dresses make their mark in another way: they cause scarring. To some brides, the scars on their hips are badges of honour, shown off to friends and show-cased on social websites. There's even a traveller saying 'The more you bleed, the better the dress.'

'I've been shown scars three or four inches long,' says Thelma, 'but they all say it was worth it.'

The cornerstone to Thelma's success is secrecy. And not just about cost. Brides are desperate for their wedding styles, themes and colours to be kept a secret from rival brides. Sometimes even the bridesmaids are barred from seeing the wedding dress until the day itself. This water-tight security is in place for one reason – sabotage.

One of Thelma's designers, blonde Leanne, is shocked by the devious antics of some rival brides. 'It is very secret-ive. We have code names for things when they are ringing up in case other people phone up and pretend to be them. People do that to try to find out what their dress is like, what their colours or themes are. I don't know where it all comes from. I don't know why they are like that. Some of them can be quite malicious really and cancel wedding dresses and things like that on behalf of someone else. It is quite shocking.

'We have had girls crying because somebody has phoned up and cancelled the wedding reception, or sabotaged a wedding by telling the venue that it's a gypsy wedding so that the venue cancels. These are girls who don't want other weddings to be as good as theirs. It is just totally crazy.'

'You come here and you're asked, "What's your dream?" Your fantasy, really. Then that's what you shall have, 'cos you only get married once!'

Inside Thelma's dream factory, we regularly get to see just what the wedding dress means to a traveller bride. Today, Bridget Ward and her best woman, Elizabeth Doran, arrive for a final fitting, a week before Bridget's wedding. This will be Elizabeth's first time out of mourning black since the death of her dad, Larry, almost a year ago.

As Thelma adds the finishing touches to their dresses in the back area of the shop, the nineteen-year-old friends from Wiltshire twitch nervously. Sure enough, Elizabeth looks sombre in black jacket and trousers. Bridget – slender, blonde, pretty – wears a metal-studded strapless black top and black jeans. It's a show of sartorial support for her grieving friend.

As they wait, the air bristles with anticipation. They're not just anxious about the dresses, though. Bridget is terrified that, after all this effort and expense, she won't be able to have a wedding reception at all. So far, three venues have cancelled her reception because they've found out she's a traveller.

Elizabeth reveals how it typically plays out. 'Couple of places, they paid a deposit and when they went to pay the full money, they handed the money straight back into his hand and said, "We can't do business with you."'

Bridget wishes they'd give her family a chance. 'If they just stopped and got to know us, instead of putting us down so low, they'd realise we're not bad people or anything.'

With days to go, Bridget's reception hangs by a thread. She's used a gorger connection to book a local golf and bowls club. The venue doesn't know it's a traveller wedding. It's a high-risk strategy. The club could find out the truth at any moment and cancel, like the others, but it is Bridget's only hope.

Sadly, both girls are seasoned victims of racism. 'They call you "gypos" and they look at you like "Oh, you're gypsy scum,"' says Elizabeth. 'Call you all sorts of names for nothing. How can they judge you if they don't know you? They chuck us out of places and they don't give a reason. There is no reason, just that we're travellers.'

At least here, at Nico, the girls are VIPs.

Elizabeth is trying to keep her fretful friend upbeat. 'Seeing the dresses today will take a lot of the pressure off,' she says brightly. 'A dress that leaves you scars!' she goes on. 'A dress that you can't fit in the door of your reception. Yeah? The bigger the dress, the better! That's the way everyone is looking at it. It's the happiest day of your life, isn't it? You gotta make the most of it.'

Bridget laughs. 'It's like you come here and you're asked, "What's your dream?" Your fantasy, really. Then that's what you shall have, 'cos you only get married once!'

Nevertheless, Bridget's nerves won't loosen their grip. 'I'm worried and excited at the same time,' she says. 'What if it doesn't turn out the way I want them to be? If they don't look the way I want, I'll be very upset.'

Elizabeth tells her she'll speak up. 'Oh, I'd come out with it. I won't hide it. No point saying you like it when you don't. I won't even put it on if we don't like it.'

Thelma's nerves are rattling too. She knows Elizabeth will speak her mind. The best woman has been instrumental in the entire wedding. She's even designed the bridesmaids' dresses herself. As Thelma says, 'The bride herself doesn't seem to have as much say as what Elizabeth has. I think sometimes she thinks she's the groom. Elizabeth basically tells you exactly what she wants and I don't think she's even interested in the bride's dress, as long as hers is OK.'

It is time. The girls are led into the inner sanctum of Nico. Their matching black outfits seem alien and cold against this kaleidoscopic dress-scape, but the girls' faces are aglow, kids on Christmas morning.

The first to get fitted is Elizabeth. She is unveiled in a shocking-pink and black bridesmaid dress, complete with pink fingerless gloves and headpiece. For a second, she seems to suck the light out of the rest of the space. Set against her jet-black hair and green eyes, it is hard to imagine anything more dramatic. For once, Elizabeth's speechless; her smile says all she needs to say.

'What do you think, Bridget? Gorgeous, isn't it?' says Thelma.

'Yeah, it really is,' says Bridget.

Now it is Bridget's turn. Once fitted, she turns impatiently to a full-length mirror. Her eyes fix hard on her own reflection. They hunt up and down. Then they soften, almost drift. Her slow, unconscious smile seems to say, 'All your dreams can come true.'

Eventually, she comes round. 'Oh, the back is fabulous,' says Bridget absently, to no one in particular. 'How gorgeous.' She looks sensational. By traveller standards, her dress is small. The top half is tight and tastefully covered in shimmering silver leaves. The bottom half is traditional, save for a handful of pretty diamond leaf designs.

Elizabeth looks on, a little rueful. 'We had this thing,' says Elizabeth, watching Bridget watching herself in the mirror. 'We used to say, "Who gets married first?" And she kept saying, "Ah, you're gonna get married first!" And I said, "No, you are!" And she goes, "I won't get married till you get married!" But she ended up getting married first.'

Bridget is transfixed, oblivious. All of her dreams have led to this single moment. 'How nice it's come out . . . I'm so happy now. I just don't want to take it off now. I just want to leave it on.'

'You can't have her plugged into the socket, obviously, because she is not going to be able to move. How is she going to dance with a big extension cable coming out the back of her dress?'

However, as one client goes away happy, another sets Thelma Madine and her team a unique challenge that is stretching even their improvisational heroics.

Sam Norton, seventeen, isn't a traveller, but she's buying into their fashion sense wholesale. Sam, who is marrying twenty-year-old gypsy tree surgeon Pat Skye Lee, wants to out-traveller the travellers by wearing a dress with special powers.

Thelma explains, 'She wants to be known as the girl whose dress lit up. She wants this dress to light up no matter what, so we have got to try and find a way of making this dress light up without setting her on fire.'

Sam's wedding dress is already unique. It is huge. And pink. And it has metallic butterflies all over it that actually flutter in the breeze.

'I don't know if she is trying to fit in,' says Thelma, 'but when she walks in wearing this dress, she may look more of a traveller than any traveller.'

'I'm wearing the dress obviously for myself, because I love to be different,' explains Sam, the rebel. 'I don't like to be the same as everybody else, and I'd like Pat to cry when I walk down the aisle.'

Pat may cry, but Sam wants to impress – and the way to do that is to bring on the pyrotechnics. As soon as darkness falls, all the venue's lights are to be extinguished so that Sam can make her entrance – lit up like a Christmas tree in her firefly dress.

Thelma's challenge is to make sure the dress lights up, not the bride. To her, it's become a recurring Wicker Woman nightmare. She says, 'We have spent a lot of time trying to find lights that will light the dress up without being dangerous as well. I have spoken to a lot of electricians all saying that it can't be done. I say, "Never say never!" because we are not going to give up. Somehow we will make that dress light up.'

They've run through various options.

Electricity: 'You can't have her plugged into the socket, obviously, because she is not going to be able to move. How is she going to dance with a big extension cable coming out the back of her dress?'

Batteries: 'You are looking at three car batteries. Sam will do anything. Even if she has to put the battery pack on a trolley and pull it behind her, she'd do it. She doesn't care. She wants this dress to light up no matter what, but I think that would look terrible.'

Gorger Sam is simply determined to outshine all her traveller counterparts. 'If Thelma can get this to work, it'll be a dream come true.'

In terms of transport for her big day, Sam is fulfilling an ancient wedding tradition. She has something old, something new, something borrowed (for borrowed, read hired) and something blue. Something old – she and her twenty-stone, high-voltage dress are being hauled to the church in a fairy-tale carriage, identical to the one Jordan had on her wedding day. Something new – Pat and pals are being ferried to the ceremony in a large red monster truck, worth £250,000 and boasting a flashing dance floor, a bar and a dancing pole. Something blue – Sam's bridesmaids are being transported in a Playboy bus, complete with dance floor, bar and shower.

'People round here just have a normal boring wedding,' says Sam, sounding more like a traveller by the day. 'We're going for it. I've dreamed of it since childhood, so why not?'

However, not all Sam's plans are working out. 'I can't find bridesmaids' dresses,' she explains. 'It's doing me head in because I've been looking everywhere. We've been to Warrington, Liverpool, Wigan. The bridesmaids can't agree on colours or style. Some want short, and some want long. I can't have them walking down the aisle in all different dresses; that'd make me look stupid.'

This is one style war with heavy casualties. Sam started off with nine albeit bickering bridesmaids. She's since been shedding them at an alarming rate.

'I keep getting texts, like, randomly: "Sorry, I can't be a bridesmaid." It's up to them, isn't it? They don't want to be one, it's their loss, so they can kiss me ass.'

Sam Norton now has two bridesmaids. Her incendiary wedding plans haven't blinded her to what she is most looking forward to about marriage – cooking and cleaning for Pat.

She says, 'I'm most looking forward to cooking a meal

and that in me own space, like, for when he gets home from work. And cleaning the trailer. I'll be able to, like, appreciate it because it's mine.'

> 'I love my dress and I bet you, take my word, there will be loads of girls copying my dress. Loads.'

It's a bright summer's day in Eastcote, West London. The McFadden girls are making their regular pilgrimage to the sunbeds when they walk past a wedding shop. In the window hangs what settled society considers a traditional white wedding dress. One of the girls asks bride-to-be Josie if she'd ever consider a dress like that. Her reaction is almost violent.

'My dress is nothing like that,' the Irish traveller, just turned seventeen, spits in disgust. 'I wouldn't wear that to a dogfight. I would die before I put that on. I'd prefer to get married in my own clothes than in that.'

Sharp-tongued Barbara, her sister, is equally scathing. 'It's like grandma's curtain net with a few diamonds stuck on.'

Josie is indignant. 'My dress is a hundred, thousand, million times better. On my wedding day, if someone was standing beside me wearing that dress, they would look like a guest.'

Josie reiterates just how important a dramatic and unique wedding dress is to a traveller bride. 'The wedding dress is the main thing out of it all. It's the biggest single thing because every girl wants their dress to be the best. You've waited since you were a baby just to wear it, to feel like a princess, like Cinderella. I love my dress and I bet you, take my word, there will be loads of girls copying my dress. Loads. I will have been the first to have it. Then people will say, "They're copying Josie."'

'Your dress is a trademark really,' explains Barbara. 'It must be something unique that you will be remembered for.'

With just days to go until the wedding, Josie can finally describe her mould-breaking dress without fear of imitation by a copycat bride. Only she can do it justice, in her own words. 'It is a big sticky-out white dress. It is really, really big. I tried it on the other day and my hips went numb. It will leave scars on my hips. They say that the more it bleeds, the better the dress.'

Now Josie reveals the single feature that makes her dress a 'first' for a traveller. 'There is a split right up the middle. You can see my legs and my garter. Then I have got a tiny pair of white diamond shorts underneath. Then where the split is, there are all Spanish frills. Nobody has ever done the split before, but it looks amazing.'

Josie reveals that her inspiration for the thigh-high split and the frills comes from Spanish flamenco. The influence for her corset comes from someone much closer to home.

'I don't know if you remember Jordan's? Well, it is a see-through corset like that with all diamonds coming down the bones of the corset. More diamonds than Jordan. You can't see anything – it is all Swarovski diamonds.'

Josie is pretty confident of where her dress sits in the pantheon of big fat gypsy dresses. 'My dress is going to be the most different one ever, the one where everyone goes, "Wow, where did you get that idea from?"'

Josie is having nine bridesmaids, all in bright pink. Or, as Swanley describes it, 'the pink that makes you blind'. They too will sport a Spanish-themed rose in their hair and daring splits up the middle of their skirts. The pink theme continues with the male wedding party. The best man and eight ushers are wearing grey suits with white shirts, pink ties and pink-and-white waistcoats. Swanley refuses to wear pink. Resistance, though, is futile. This wedding is pinker than Barbara Cartland.

While Josie plans to arrive at the church in a white Rolls-Royce Phantom, the rest of the McFadden party are being transported in two twenty-seat Hummers, white but with pink interiors. The entire reception hall is being decked out in pink balloons, ribbons and flowers. The napkins are pink origami roses. The pink rose theme extends to the enormous cake. The main part has six tiers, white but covered in pink roses. The main cake is connected to lots of smaller cakes by an elaborate network of bridges spanning little waterfalls. One of these sub-cakes is a white-and-pink Bible with a pink rose in each corner and the words 'God bless, for ever happy, Swanley and Josie' in pink. All this is topped off by four trays of cupcakes, iced, needless to say, with pink roses.

At least they now have a venue to turn pink.

'How much torture was it?' Josie says. 'I was crying down the phone every day going, "We are never going to get one!"'

Several hotels took a deposit only to then turn away the booking. Some pretended that they had suddenly become fully booked. Others just messed the couple about.

Like most travellers, though, Josie and Swanley seem remarkably sanguine in the face of naked racism. Maybe they're used to it.

'I suppose it is a bit weird,' says Swanley, 'but in their eyes they think, Oh my God, travellers! There is going to be a fight or a riot. Do you know what I mean? Half the time they are right,' he laughs. 'No, honestly, there is hardly any trouble. And if there is, it doesn't happen inside the place. There's never trouble inside.'

'I just think that when you say "traveller" or "gypsy", I think it just scares them,' says Josie. 'When travellers have a wedding, everyone always thinks there are going to be murders or fighting and whatnot.'

Finally, Josie figured out a sure-fire way to secure a licensed premises. 'They don't know that I am a traveller. I had to go in and put on a really posh English voice.'

Josie has outfoxed any would-be saboteurs planning to tip off the venue. The reception's location is a secret known only to her and her parents. The address will be revealed on the morning of the wedding.

'Some girls will ring up that are jealous,' she says. 'Or if you have had an argument with them, they will ring up and cancel it or ring up and tell the venue that you are gypsies. Then it just gets cancelled.'

Josie's terror is that the venue will find out through other sources – or cancel the wedding on the day itself, once they realise it's a traveller do. 'Sometimes they do that – call the police and hand you your money back – and you standing there in your wedding dress,' she says.

'Some girls will ring up that are jealous. Or if you have had an argument with them, they will ring up and cancel it or ring up and tell the venue that you are gypsies. Then it just gets cancelled.'

Meanwhile, in Cheshire, it's the eve of Cindy McDonagh's spectacular wedding to Irish traveller and Kevin Bacon lookalike Johnny. Twenty-one-year-old Cindy has given wedding planner Gaynor a simple but daunting brief: 'She wants everybody to say her wedding was the best that they have ever been to.'

Cindy has been dating her fiancé Johnny for three years. This has given her plenty of time to dream up every gimmick possible for her nuptials. Cindy knows exactly what she wants, 'down to the last detail'. And money is no object.

The venue: a glorious country-house estate in the North-West of England. The owner refuses to let us identify the location. He's worried that hosting a traveller wedding might lessen its allure to footballers, soap stars and any other celebrity racists. Weather permitting, the ceremony will be outdoors.

The entrance: Cindy has booked a helicopter. She wants her entrance to be unforgettable, except she's not arriving in the chopper. She explains her expensive ruse: 'I want the excitement of everyone thinking that it's me coming when they see the helicopter, but then they'll be thinking, Hang on, where's the groom? The groom's not there! They'll all be thinking, How shameful – he's not turning up and here comes the bride. And then when he gets out, they are all going to be relieved, aren't they? The groom has arrived!' Cindy will then come galloping round the corner in a traditional horse and carriage.

The owl: the wedding ceremony has a feature that wedding-planner Gaynor has never seen or even heard of before. The rings are being delivered to the best man at the altar by an owl named Spirit. Gaynor prays that the bird of prey delivers. 'If it's raining and we have it inside, the room has a low ceiling and a lot of beams. I worry that it'll fly into a beam and kill itself. As for outside, I just hope they've trained the owl properly, because if it goes flying off with the ring, it will either be very funny or a nightmare.'

The thrones: à la Posh and Becks, Cindy and Johnny will sit through their ceremony on two enormous silver thrones.

The mini-man: to liven up the meal, Cindy has hired what she and Gaynor call a 'mini-man'. Gaynor tries to explain what the mini-man will actually do: 'It is a small guy that is going to be dressed up and he is going to be running around all of the tables. I am not too sure what he is dressing up in, but I think it might be a leprechaun. It was Cindy's idea. The DJ has a special tune for him to run around to.'

The dance floor: Cindy is having a customised LED dance floor installed in the reception room that flashes in time with the music.

The free bar: Cindy – a born-again Christian – had originally planned a dry wedding. Then her dad persuaded her to acknowledge her Christian beliefs and her traveller heritage by putting on a free bar from 7 p.m. onwards. Cindy explains, 'I want me whole wedding to represent

God. More than anything. I want people to feel Jesus. A full-on Christian wedding has no alcohol, but I have to be fair because I have to think about the rest of the guests as well.'

The cake: according to the delightful Irish traveller Noreen from ABC Cakes, Cindy's is 'a horse-and-carriage theme, with waterfalls and Bibles. Peach. Oh, and hearts. And doves.' Noreen approves. 'It was her idea. She is dead proud of that moment. The traveller brides, they want to bring out a new fashion. Now Cindy's just bought out a new fashion with a horse-and-carriage cake. I've never seen that before.'

Noreen – a traveller-wedding veteran – is already calling this 'the Traveller Wedding of the Year'. For Cindy, this kind of hype heaps on the pressure.

'Everything is worrying in case it don't go the right way,' she says. 'I never stopped going the whole day, driving back and forward, back and forward, picking up suits, picking up underskirts, picking up the bridesmaid dresses, picking up the bridesmaids' shoes, picking up the bridesmaids' jewellery. I haven't got my dress yet, I haven't got my jewellery, I haven't got my shoes, and I need a helium bottle.'

Groom Johnny and his party are taking an altogether more relaxed approach – and it's starting to rankle. 'They had their suit fitting three days ago,' says Cindy, 'and they never even went for that.'

'The men don't really have to do anything,' says Cindy's mum, Margaret. 'They've got to wear a shirt and a tie, a suit. That's it.'

Cindy admits she's done almost everything for her husband-to-be. 'I picked out everything for Johnny apart from his shoes. But his mum got his shoes for him.'

Cindy has learned a big lesson over the last few weeks. 'The boys just want everything to be over and done with as quickly as possible, but the girl doesn't really want their big day to end. They generally want to capture every moment of the fairy tale. In *Cinderella*, you barely see Prince Charming, do you? They just can't be bothered.'

Meanwhile, Prince Charming's busy chilling with the boys. Johnny tells them how he feels about the big day tomorrow. 'For me, the day is about getting drunk. To be honest, I am nervous about everything. It is all embarrassing, with everyone focusing on you. You know?'

His best man sympathises. 'Men are not interested about the wedding. The woman makes all of the arrangements, designs everything.'

Johnny, the sage, says it's better for all this way. 'There's no arguments then. It just makes life an awful lot easier.'

However, Johnny acknowledges that the wedding day is a major milestone in both his and Cindy's life because after tomorrow, he's the boss. 'Well, I'll be in charge after that. It's weird – it changes a lot. Big responsibility. It's a big step for both of us, you know. I'll be responsible for her from now on, not her dad. The boy is the head of the home, you know? The woman is just in charge of cleaning, looking after the men, pampering them, washing them, feeding them.'

He laughs, but you sense he isn't joking.

'The child don't understand . . . I'm gonna cry a river.'

For traveller girls, getting married means leaving home. To understand how big a step this is for these young women, you first have to appreciate just how close and interdependent most traveller families are. Traveller girls are with their mums and sisters all day, every day. They don't go anywhere without them. The traveller sisters in *BFGW* are inseparable. If a traveller girl doesn't have a sister, or if her sisters have moved away, she finds a substitute sister: Cheyenne and Montana Pidgley; Bridget Ward and Elizabeth Doran. They are as close as any biological sisters.

Because traveller families tend to be big, older sisters play a major role in bringing up younger siblings. Some are virtual mums to brothers and sisters. Older brothers protect and look out for their sisters. As you've read in previous chapters, traveller girls sometimes need a boy on their side.

Then there's the daddy-daughter relationship. Traveller dads seem to adore and cherish their daughters. They want to protect them at all costs from potential harm. To settled families, some traveller dads may seem overprotective and overbearing, but traveller girls seem universally devoted to their daddies.

Most *BFGW* brides have never been away from their families before. Those who have spent a night, maybe two, with a grandparent, and often they hated it.

As their wedding day approaches, traveller girls tend to be consumed by conflicting emotions. On one hand, their dreams are about to come true. Cinderella is going to the ball. No more cleaning up after siblings and worrying about your good name. Relative freedom. They can drink, smoke, go to nightclubs, have sex. On the other hand, the girls are leaving the only life they know. They are moving away from all the people they love in the world, bar one, to live on a traveller site full of strangers, sometimes hundreds of miles away. They are often too young to drive. Their new husband's going to be out at work all day. It's like they go from chaos to isolation in twenty-four hours flat.

Tomorrow, Lizzie Lee will become a married woman. The Vivaldi trailer she's loved and scrubbed all these years will be hers. Her new life with Johnny will be in Watford, on the other side of London.

She admits the thing she dreads most is leaving her three-year-old brother, Simey. 'I think I'm gonna cry, leaving Simey. It ain't hit me yet. I don't know when it will. Oh God! It's bad. The child don't understand. I've told him, but he just thinks he's coming with me. So I don't know if he'll understand when he wakes up and realises I'm not here. I'm gonna cry a river.'

Lizzie Lee has lived on this site for ten years. Like all of us, she fears the unknown.

'I don't know what to expect, like, and how different it's gonna be. I don't know how long it's gonna take me to get used to living somewhere different and waking up with peace and quiet, not three children screaming all over the place. I'm nervous, worried, excited all at the same time. I think the happiest moment about tomorrow will be getting ready. The rest of it . . . I'm just shaking.'

> 'I'm nervous, worried, excited all at the same time. I think the happiest moment about tomorrow will be getting ready. The rest of it . . . I'm just shaking.'

Romany gypsy Violet Anne Stubley is about to quit her job as a hotel receptionist. Next week, after her wedding to fellow gypsy Larry, she's moving from her family home in Leicestershire to a site in Slough, Berkshire, over a hundred miles away.

Unlike lots of gypsy and traveller girls, Violet Anne loves the freedom that comes with earning her own money. 'Once I've got my own money, I can do my own thing. I can go and do what I want then.'

Her boss and colleagues at the hotel have no idea that their bright, straight-talking receptionist has harboured a secret all these years – she's a Romany gypsy. In fact, gypsies have been frequently turned away from the hotel.

Violet Anne describes having to sit silently while colleagues derided her culture. 'When the gypsies are on the premises,' she reveals, 'they always say, "Do not let them in." I think if they ever knew I was a gypsy, I'd be straight out the door.'

Yet Violet Anne has an impeccable five-year record working here. As she says, 'I've shown that I can be responsible, trustworthy, reliable. I'm always on time. I've handled large sums of cash. Never a problem.'

Violet Anne's a proud Romany, keen to relieve herself of the weighty secret she's kept for so long. 'It's time to tell them I'm a gypsy, see the expressions on their faces. I want them to learn that there is good and bad in everyone, not to class everyone as the same.'

Violet Anne has waited until her very last shift to tell her boss her secret. She has always feared a backlash. Now it doesn't matter. 'If they do say anything what's not nice, I can just say, "There's your job. There's your keys back. I'm off." End of story. I will be upset, but that's why I've left it to the last day. I won't need the job any longer.'

Later that evening, her boss, Sunni, pays tribute to his loyal receptionist. He says, 'Violet's been with us since 2005. She's always been reliable. I'll be sad to see her go. Violet works here on her own, so I'm trusting her with the whole hotel really. I can always rely on her. But I want to wish her luck in her new life.'

Violet Anne picks this moment to drop her bombshell. 'Sunni's going to be a bit shocked when I tell him that I'm going to live in a caravan.'

She's wrong. Sunni isn't a bit shocked; he's gobsmacked. Visibly shaken, he utters an incredulous 'What?'

Despite her fighting talk earlier, Violet Anne is trembling. 'He don't know. I've never told him this before. I'm a gypsy.'

Sunni is flummoxed. 'You what? Bloody hell!'

Violet Anne tells Sunni that he shouldn't make judgements about people until he knows them. Sunni's still too shocked to see the broader picture.

'Bloody hell,' he says again. 'I didn't know that. You shocked me there a bit.'

It takes Sunni several minutes to recover. When he does, he concedes he's been taught a valuable lesson. 'Everyone's got the prejudgement of gypsies. This has changed my opinion of gypsies. Like I said, she's reliable and trustworthy. Violet's ticked all the boxes on that.'

She doesn't, however, tick all the *Big Fat Gypsy Wedding* boxes, as she later tells us. Feisty Violet Anne has shunned a fat frock in favour of an off-the-hanger number.

'It's not fifty stone and twenty stone and all that,' she states bluntly. 'It's just right. I can walk in it. It's just comfortable. I'd rather be plainer than big and tacky. I'm not having a big frock, and I'm not having a big, spectacular do, just a normal wedding.'

Violet Anne is on tack alert – she can't abide bad taste, anything over the top or tacky. She has, however, permitted herself one monster indulgence – a six-foot cake.

'I'm only five foot one. I can't wait to see it, but I hope it's not way too big. I hope it doesn't look tacky, 'cos if it looks tacky, I'll cry my eyes out. I don't know, I'll smash it to pieces.'

Like many of the betrothed in *BFGW*, Violet Anne reveals this will be her first time away from her parents. 'I wasn't even allowed to dances or to have a night out. I never left me mum and dad, never, so that is going to kill me. I dread it. Me nieces and nephews have always been with me; they are more like me brothers and sisters. Not having them close, that is going to just do me head in.'

> 'I've done weddings before for travellers and it's kicked off.'

There are three Bridgets having big fat gypsy weddings. The first is Bridget Ward – the nineteen-year-old from Wiltshire who fears she may not get to have a reception at all. The second Bridget is another slim, blue-eyed, blonde Irish traveller, but from Lincolnshire. Bridget Rooney hit on her unique wedding theme as a little girl. Ever since, she's fretted that someone else would beat her to it. Now, with just weeks to go, Bridget Rooney knows she's setting a traveller first. She's turning a little corner of Lincoln into Honolulu with her tropical-themed wedding.

In many ways, Bridget Rooney's story is a mish-mash of all the others. She's always dreamed about her wedding day. She met Patrick at a wedding. Whirlwind romance. Engagement. Horse-drawn carriage. Massive do. Twenty-stone wedding dress – in fact, Bridget, in agony at her dress fitting, utters a phrase we would hear from several other wincing brides: 'Pain is beauty.' The story has a quirk, though: after their honeymoon in Egypt, Bridget and Patrick are moving to the US. So an emotional day beckons for all.

Where Bridget Rooney's story is also different is that we get to see a traveller wedding from the point of view of a hotel hosting the reception. With so many traveller brides getting blown out by venues, we want to see a big fat gypsy wedding from the perspective of hotel staff and management.

Introducing Mandy, general manager, and Will, deputy manager, at the Pride of Lincoln. The first thing both admit is they don't want the booking.

Mandy says, 'If I had originally been here, I probably

wouldn't have taken the booking, because I've done weddings before for travellers and it's kicked off. The reason I haven't walked away is because it's there now and I've got to deal with it, and I think the outcome now will be absolutely fantastic.'

However, Mandy has laid down rigid ground rules for the Rooneys. In case their guests don't comply, she's drafted in additional security. 'We've made it clear that 1 a.m. is time and not any longer. At the end of the day, they're going to be drinking for nine hours. We haven't brought doormen in as such, but there is extra security.'

Will says that marathon boozing is the primary source of aggro at all their functions. The fact that the Rooneys are travellers changes nothing. 'Just because of who they are, I don't think that makes it any different. You always have a doubt in your mind because of drinking, and an action plan in place for a scuffle. We are all human beings; it happens to everybody, at even the poshest dos. We have it all in place. I think if there is a glitch, we can have it fixed instantly.'

Will says he feels that a lot of the negative attitudes towards travellers are misplaced. As far as he is concerned, this is just another wedding. 'The vibe we get from the family is a positive vibe and it'll be a day they'll remember for the rest of their lives.'

Mandy is reassured by the dignity of Bridget's family. 'We've seen so much of Bridget and her mum, and had so many conversations. We know they don't want any trouble,' she says. 'They said to me if there's anybody in the room they don't want, who do they come to? We said come to us and she's happy with that, so we're all happy. It's about respect and they're a very respectable family.'

Both Will and Mandy marvel at the transformation of their function room into a tropical paradise. It's the first time they've seen it covered floor to ceiling in flowers, trees, lights, balloons and ribbons. The six-foot-wide cake with castle, waterfall and light-up cathedral is 'unlike anything we've seen before'. And it's the first time they've laid on a red-carpet champagne greeting for arriving guests.

All twenty bedrooms here are taken for the night. Three large nearby hotels are booked out. Will admits, 'It's the biggest we've done. They've just gone all out and it feels like a celebrity wedding on a smaller scale. It's going to be special.'

Mandy is excited but nervous. 'I've got butterflies because nothing will please me more than when they leave here to go and catch a plane for their honeymoon and wave goodbye and we see the smiles on them faces.'

Their first surprise was meeting a sixteen-year-old bride with a clear Hollywood-director vision of exactly what she wants.

Mandy reveals, 'She knew before she walked in the door what cake she wanted, colour scheme, dress. She's probably been planning this since she was about eight or nine years old. It's a little girl's dream, isn't it? A fairy-tale.'

Will says Bridget's the youngest bride he's ever dealt with. 'The pressure is mounting on Bridget and we're beginning to see the panic in her eyes. It's very difficult at such a young age to take so much on her shoulders.'

Her first request had been for security for her unique

wedding outfits. Even at this late stage, Bridget Rooney wants nothing to leak out about her tropical-themed brides-maids' dresses.

Will says, 'They're locked away. We know it's very import-ant to Bridget. We were instructed to be the only people who can see the dresses.'

As part of her tropical theme, Bridget wants to enter the reception, post-meal, to reggae music. In keeping with traveller tradition, Bridget has hand-picked songs for her 'farewell' wedding dance with her dad, then her mum, then her siblings. For Bridget's family, this really is goodbye. Next day, she leaves the country for good.

'There won't be a dry eye in the house,' Mandy sighs.

> 'She knew before she walked in the door what cake she wanted, colour scheme, dress. She's probably been planning this since she was about eight or nine years old. It's a little girl's dream, isn't it? A fairy-tale.'

The third bride named Bridget is Bridget Doran, nineteen, from Wolverhampton. Next week, she marries Irish travel-ler Tommy, seventeen, from Dudley.

Bridget and her mum are on their way to Nico in Liverpool for the unveiling of her wedding dress. She is a doe-eyed, dark-skinned brunette, pretty but with strong, striking features and a soft voice. Compared to the other

A girl in a traditional Romany caravan at Stow Fair in the Cotswolds, which draws 10,000 gypsies and travellers each year

A man relaxes at Stow Fair

Boys with their horses at a Fair

The Fairs are enjoyed by young and old alike

Girls and boys socialise at
Appleby Fair

Most of the girls pull
out all the stops to
look good

Young men keen to
show off their lean
physiques

Horses are taken into Appleby's River Eden to drink

The old gypsy way of life is changing – modern new caravans are gradually replacing the traditional Romany caravans

Girls dressed to impress

Irish traveller girls we met, Bridget seems withdrawn, a little introverted.

She's another traveller who's never been away from her mother before, even for a single night. Leaving home seems alien. 'I feel strange. Me and my mum are really close. We are always doing things together, and we are always going everywhere together. I have never been away from her. She will just get lonesome. Like, I would be very lonesome on my own as well.'

This is a Cinderella story with a twist. Their unbreakable bond has been forged out of terror. Bridget's mum is one of the few traveller women we met who has left her husband – and she was forced to do so because of his violence and abuse. Bridget, the oldest of four siblings, was just six when they fled from her dad.

'The best thing I ever done was to take me kids out of that marriage and rear them on me own, stop them looking at the violence,' says Bridget Senior. 'I got married, I was only young, and the marriage was perfect at first, but then my husband started drinking and things started getting really bad. I just left him. Just too much fighting. It was too violent. Just up and gone. There comes a time when you have to do it. I went to me mum and dad's, and then they sorted me out with a caravan, clothes for the kids, and travelled around with me, just keep me away, like, hiding me out, because he was a violent man. And then I got a divorce.'

Thelma, busy adding the finishing touches to Bridget's dress – another diamond-splattered whopper – knows the backstory well. 'Bridget Senior is one of the most remarkable women in the travelling community, and one of the nicest. She is divorced from the dad, which is very, very unusual in the traveller community. She went through a very abusive relationship and she got out of it. She's brought up all the children on her own. She's done a really good job. I know that Bridget does a lot of the work for her mum because she's got arthritis in her hands and legs and finds it difficult to walk. They are really, really close. I don't think I've ever seen a mum and daughter so close. They get on so well.'

Later, Thelma unveils Bridget Doran Junior in her fairy-tale frock. Bridget Senior struggles to hold back tears. 'When she was small, younger, I tried to be a mum and dad to her. Trying to give her the very best, give her as good as the next girl had. It's been hard, it's been a rough road, but I got there in the end for her. Do you know what I mean? I am very proud of her, very, very proud of her, and I'm very proud of what I achieved for Bridget.'

The pioneering mum is doing this for Bridget because she has a special message for her oldest child. She says, 'There is something I want to say and that is thank you. Since she was a baby it was always me and you. But it is really to say thank you for being a good daughter and being there whenever I need you. I'm crying now.'

As the camera pans around the room, everyone's in tears.

CHAPTER EIGHT

The Big Days

*'You haven't lived until you've been to
a traveller wedding ...'*

'I do', the two words that cause so much time, effort and money to be invested. So how do the big fat gypsy wedding days turn out? There are, of course, acres of dress fabric and buckets of tears, of joy and sorrow. The big fat gypsy weddings also feature a hotel eviction. A couple of punch-ups. Plenty of grabbing. And some of the brides and grooms very nearly don't make it at all. In this chapter, we float from wedding to wedding to present snapshots of the dramas at each do. So, ladies and gentlemen, please be upstanding for the three Bridgets – Ward, Rooney and Doran – Josie McFadden, Lizzie Lee, Cindy McDonagh, Violet Anne Stubley and Sam Norton.

'They wanted them thrown out because they probably heard that we're travellers again. They're racist again. That's all.'

It's the night before nineteen-year-old Bridget Ward's wedding to Patrick. Inside her trailer in deepest Wiltshire, she and her best woman, Elizabeth Doran, are busy shoving endless underskirts and bridesmaids' dresses into bags. They're bringing the wedding frocks to a hotel in Swindon where they're sharing a room tonight. Tomorrow morning, the eight other bridesmaids will join them to get ready for the big day.

Bridget seems preoccupied, worried. Three venues cancelled her reception when they found out she's a traveller, so she hasn't told the golf and bowls club she's booked that it's a traveller wedding. She's terrified they will find out and pull the plug, even at this late stage.

As her friend Elizabeth says, 'I wouldn't say she's worried about getting married at all. She's very nervous about the venue working out. As soon as they see we're travellers, they could pull down the shutters and call the police. Wedding day over.'

It is 11 p.m. when Bridget gets a call on her mobile phone. She looks horrified at what she's hearing. When, finally, the call ends, Bridget explains what's happened: wedding guests had booked en masse to stay at a hotel in Swindon, but now they're being made to leave.

'Over at the hotel, everyone is getting thrown out,' she reveals. 'All the children, all in their pyjamas, getting thrown out with their mums and dads 'cos all the children were making noise, yeah. It's outrageous. They threw them out. They're in the car park now, all over the kids making noise. I don't understand it. They're not teenagers; they are only kids – five and six, and a newborn baby.'

Elizabeth is horrified. 'A baby, a baby was thrown out into a car park? No way!'

'Yeah, she got fired out,' says Bridget. 'Eileen told me, "Oh, they're shutting all of the showers." They're all out in the car park in dressing gowns with rollers in their hair. The police come to the door. This is all because the children was making noise. They wanted them thrown out because they probably heard that we're travellers again. They're racist again. That's all.'

Now the evicted travellers have to find somewhere else to sleep at this late hour.

'Let's hope to God it don't happen tomorrow at the reception,' the bride says grimly.

Bridget, usually so serene, is frazzled. 'Me brain's all messed up. I don't know if I'm thinking straight. My mind's on a different world. Do you know what I mean? People is talking to me and I'm like, "What?" Do you know what I mean? And then for this to happen . . .'

Elizabeth, Bridget's rock, melts away. 'I don't know what to say. How can you take the worry off her?'

'I'm not there, Josie isn't there, and we have got half an hour to go and it takes half an hour to get there.'

It's the morning of Josie McFadden's wedding day to Swanley Smith. At the hotel in West London where she and her family are staying, merry chaos reigns.

Bride-to-be Josie is in high spirits. 'Oh my God! I am getting married,' she squeals. 'I have got excitement in my stomach. I want to scream! Like, I don't know whether to cry or laugh. I feel like I have got all these butterflies in my stomach and they are just flying around. "Is this really happening?" kind of thing.'

A little later, her mood needle swings completely the other way. 'I know my daddy will be crying. I know that when I leave the reception, he will be crying his heart out because I was his first child, and as he always says, he fell in love with one Josie, my mummy, and then he found me and fell in love with another Josie. He calls me after the first woman that he fell in love with. He never wants to see me leave. If I could get married and live in the same house as Daddy, then he wouldn't mind then, but it doesn't work like that.'

Barbara, her fourteen-year-old sister, brings Josie sharply back to the present. 'Honestly, no way in the world am I having a wedding like yours,' she moans. 'Too much hassle.'

Josie hits back, mood swing number three. 'It's your job as best woman to make sure it all goes smoothly. It better or I am going to murder you.'

'I am going to be all right,' Barbara teases. 'It is Swanley that you have to worry about, Josie.'

'Swanley will be there!' says Josie.

Barbara's turning the screw. 'Are you sure? What if he gets cold feet on the way? Josie is standing at the aisle wondering if he is going to come.'

'He will be there,' Josie shouts, stopping this line of banter stone dead.

At 11.30 a.m., Swanley - dapper in a grey suit - sets off in his white van for the church in Ivor, Berkshire. The church is a short drive from Swanley's hotel – if you know where you're going.

'Josie gets a limo and I get a Transit,' he quips. 'Gypsy-boy style!'

When he checks his watch, Swanley's smile disappears. 'I've got an hour and thirty-five mins. Time is pressing on now. Badly.'

An hour later, Swanley is lost. He gets a call from Josie – the limos haven't turned up for her and the bridesmaids. It is half an hour to the wedding.

'Fucking hell, it is half past twelve,' says Swanley, driving at speed. 'Well, it is twelve thirty-six – twenty-five minutes to the wedding. I'm not there, Josie isn't there, and we have got half an hour to go and it takes half an hour to get there. Jesus Christ. Nah, it is all right. The Lord will bless us. He will bless us.'

'Josie gets a limo and I get a Transit, Gypsy-boy style!'

In the sitting room of a large brick house in Wolverhampton, Thelma Madine and her assistant Pauline are on all fours, wrestling with Bridget Doran's underskirts.

At the best of times, Bridget, nineteen, seems intense. She is beautiful, with jet-black hair, big, dark eyes and immaculate olive skin, but, as ever, she looks worried. Bridget is a caring person; worrying comes with the territory.

Thelma, still at her feet, is giving her a pep talk. 'You look like Cinderella, and you *are* Cinderella for a day. This is your day, so enjoy every minute of it, babe. Probably been thinking about that since you were a little girl.'

Bridget brightens. 'I didn't even know that it was going to be a fairy-tale wedding. My mum insisted I have the big reception and cake and everything.'

The one thing missing is her father. Bridget Senior ran away with her four kids twelve years ago because of his violence and drinking.

'Me dad is not going to walk me down the aisle, so my brother Tommy is going to give me away. And me mum will have to have the first dance with me, because me dad never really reared me.'

Bridget admits she is tense. 'I am just nervous about how everything is going to go. I'm not nervous about getting married, just nervous about how everything is going to go. That's it.'

A little later, Bridget reveals that something else is on her mind. Her mum, Bridget Senior, seems anxious. 'My mum seems this morning quiet and a little on edge. It's going to be so different. I am always worried about her.'

Like the rest of the family, brother Tommy is proud of what they've achieved together without their dad. 'Her dress shows how much a success she came in life. And to let her know that people cares about her, how much her family and all that loves her. And they are all there for her on her big day. Yeah, I feel very proud of her. I'm honoured to walk her down the aisle. Her father isn't there, is he? Because he never is there. He won't even be man enough to walk her down the aisle.'

Tommy predicts a tough day for his mum. 'I bet she will be crying the whole day, yeah. Soft heart, very nice mother. She took care of us since the father left. She's a very loving mum, you know, very caring. She'll miss Bridget terrible.'

Bridget Senior seems drawn, a little pale. It's more than pre-wedding nerves. There is something on her mind. Away from everyone, she reveals what's wrong. She has heard that her violent ex-husband is planning to show up at today's wedding reception. 'At a traveller's reception, anyone can turn up. They don't have to be invited. Do you know what I mean?' she says. 'I've ordered an extra two security guards because I don't want Bridget getting upset. If her dad shows up, I just want him to be taken away. It's for her sake really. I hope he doesn't show up,' she says. 'He had his chance and he never came. He could have rung up. He could have dropped in and seen her before her wedding. He could have even given her the honour of walking her down the aisle. He never even offered to do that.'

> 'I will be most worried if, like, three thousand
> people turn up. We just don't know how many
> are going to come.'

Beaming sunshine adds yet more glamour to the country-estate setting for Cindy McDonagh's big day.

Chatty cake-maker Noreen believes this wedding will set a new benchmark for rival families. 'I mean, look at this place – a manor house. She's got a marquee. Silver thrones for the service. An owl delivering the rings. A helicopter. Horse and carriage. A lit-up dance floor. It really is like a celebrity wedding, the "Wedding of the Year" amongst travellers. It will really shock me if another traveller can beat this, because this wedding . . . wow. You'd only see it in, like, *OK!* magazine. In my eyes, it's a celebrity wedding for Cindy. To me, it's like P. Diddy. Do you know what I mean?'

Wedding planner Gaynor has been despatched by bride-to-be Cindy on a very special mission, but Gaynor's on edge. The groom has to do something all by himself. So far, Johnny hasn't had to lift a finger. Later today, he and his party have to turn up at a local airport on time, to get choppered to the ceremony. 'I'll be still anxious about the helicopter until I see it land,' she says.

Other details are nagging her. Firstly, rain is forecast. 'It's not rained on any of my brides while they've had their photographs took, so now it's become a personal challenge. I will be most worried if, like, three thousand people turn up. We just don't know how many are going to come.'

The bride, Cindy, on the other hand, is 'lovin' it'.

'At the moment, I'm at McDonald's,' says Gaynor. 'She wants me to get some food from McDonald's for her and take it to the hotel. She asked me to ring her now. I'm here to take her order.'

As she exits the drive-thru, McWedding breakfast scored, Gaynor shakes her head. 'I mean, I never, ever imagined in my life I'd get asked to go to McDonald's, but that's just the way it is.'

It's 1.15 p.m. in Manchester. Groom Johnny anxiously awaits the arrival of three members of his wedding party. They're expected at the airport by 2.15 p.m., to be flown to the wedding in time for the 2.30 p.m. start.

The groom has a question for best man Jimmy, who's playing with his iPhone – how long will it take to get to the helicopter people?

Jimmy has a confession to make. 'It'll take about . . . See, I don't know where it is, to be honest with you. That's what I'm trying to do here: find out. We should have found out where this was really. You know what I mean? We should have already had this pre-planned.'

Finally, the rest of the wedding party turns up, but Jimmy still hasn't figured out where they're going.

'We've got very little time to get there as well,' he says as they climb into the hire car.

Meanwhile, in Cindy's hotel room, the bride is ready. She's opted for traditional over big and looks radiant. The vision in white transports mum Margaret back to her own big day.

'This is better than I imagined she would look,' she says. 'She looks amazing, doesn't she? It brings back memories, as we are twenty-four years married today.'

Cindy, the organiser, is right in the present and getting antsy. 'I'm very nervous. I don't think I'm going to relax at all today. I don't really want to relax. I don't want to sit back and chill out. I want to make sure everything goes nicely.'

With so many sideshows – a dwarf entertainer, an owl, a helicopter – how will Cindy cope if something goes wrong?

'I class them as bonuses if they go right. The only thing that could spoil today is if the groom don't show up, which is doubtful. That would be the worst thing to go wrong, wouldn't it? The groom no showing and the wedding no going ahead.'

Back in Manchester, it's 1.55 p.m. Groom Johnny and the boys are doing their best not to make it. They need to land at the wedding at 2.30 p.m. They've been told the flight takes fifteen minutes. 2 p.m. is fast approaching, but they are lost.

Best man Jimmy says, 'I don't think there's a problem. He's just a bit mixed up on where he needs to take us.'

Groom Johnny is feeling it, though. 'I haven't got a clue where it is. Could end up missing me own wedding today.'

What the boys don't know is that the pilot supposed to

fly them to the wedding ceremony is under the impression that the booking's been cancelled and he's about to head home.

> 'That would be the worst thing to go wrong, wouldn't it? The groom no showing and the wedding no going ahead.'

In Lincolnshire, our second Bridget – Rooney – has married without a hitch. It might be a cold March day outside, but her tropical-theme wedding reception is hotting up. The guests, giddy with champagne, are hungry.

'The atmosphere is buzzing, absolutely buzzing,' reports Will, deputy manager of the Pride of Lincoln. 'Lots of young children – not often you see that at a wedding.'

For Will, the day's crisis point is here. They had no idea how many guests would turn up. The numbers look big. The question is, have they made enough food to feed them all? To run out of food would be mortifying for the proud Rooney clan and expensive for Will. Hungry guests equals unpaid bill.

'It's that butterfly feeling,' squeaks Will, 'that adrenaline buzz, which is why we enjoy doing what we're doing. It's getting close now. Once everyone's settled and everyone's fed, I will be happy. I've got that feeling now where it's like being stood on the side of the stage waiting to go on your first pantomime.'

Let's hope he's not about to become the pantomime

villain. As he speaks, Bridget's dad – one of the most respected traveller men in Britain – is right behind him . . .

'They'll say, "We didn't realise this is a travel-lers' do." They are going to give the deposit back, give the money back.'

Back in Swindon, it's the morning of Bridget Ward's wedding to Patrick. The management of the local golf and bowls club still don't know they're hosting a traveller wedding. The guests who were thrown out of a nearby hotel last night had no choice but to drive the seventeen miles to Bridget's site and seek beds there. Now that word is out that there's a traveller wedding in town, Bridget fears even more that the club will cancel.

'Very stressful. Very nervous,' she says. 'I never went properly to sleep. Like, I laid down about four o'clock and then I was twisting and turning.'

Guests turning up at the church are horrified to learn what happened last night. One of them is Bridget's uncle, ex-bareknuckle fighter Paddy Doherty.

'When they found out they were travellers, they phoned for the police. You don't need to phone for the police, not in this day and age. Imagine getting kids out of bed at one o'clock in the morning, throwing them out like they're nothing. They wouldn't do that to a black, would they? Or to a Pakistani or an Indian. There'd be an outcry. But when you're a gypsy or traveller, they don't give a fuck. What can she do? It's a way of life for all of us; to get kicked out of a place means nothing any more.'

Meanwhile, at the golf and bowls club in Swindon, one woman is terrified that she's about to give the game away. Gill from ABC Cakes is the first to arrive, and she's delivering what might prove the Judas kiss to Bridget's wedding reception.

Bridget has opted for a classic fairy-tale traveller cake – a pink-and-white castle with turrets, a limousine, fairy lights and lots of diamonds. Weighing about fifty kilos, the cake had to be transported here in the back of a Transit van and requires a twelve-foot table. Gill knows that the cake is a telltale sign that this is a traveller wedding. She fears that as soon as the management clap eyes on it, they'll lock the doors and call the police.

'When they see the cake, they are going to know they are travellers. It's a bit of a giveaway. It's one of those situations, you know, just play it by ear. Obviously, we can't say anything. I don't want it on my neck that I'm the person that told them. Sadly, it's happened before.'

The wedding ceremony itself goes without a hitch. Bridget leaves the church a married woman, but still fearing that she won't be allowed to celebrate the biggest day of her life simply because she's a traveller.

Thelma Madine explains what Bridget and her family are going through. 'We are just waving them off now. They are particularly worried now about going to this venue and hoping that nothing goes wrong. They are all nervous. Her mother is nervous, her sister is nervous, best woman Elizabeth is nervous, and Bridget is really nervous about it.

'I think as soon as they roll up and the people there see their outfits, then they will know that they are travellers. Whether it sets alarm bells ringing, I don't know. Some hotels are fine. This one might hand her back the deposit and call the police if they don't leave.'

Paddy describes what's happening as they leave the church in convoy. 'It's a sad thing to say, we're going to the reception and it's a fifty-fifty. If they find out we're travellers here, we're not getting in, end of story. First thing they will do is 999, get the police. They'll say, "We didn't realise this is a travellers' do." They are going to give the deposit back, give the money back.'

> 'Oh, Josie, Josie, what have you done to me? . . . I don't know, Josie, I am stressing out. Where the fuck are you?'

Back in West London, seventeen-year-old Irish traveller Josie McFadden is in a blind panic. It is twelve thirty. She is supposed to be getting married at 1 p.m. It is a half-hour journey from the hotel where she and her family are staying to the church in Ivor. On a clear run.

In the background, dad Chris can't get through to the limo company.

'No. No. No. Mother of God. We have twenty-five minutes to get there,' Josie screams.

'We shall get through this together,' laughs Barbara, cool as a breeze. 'God love her!'

Meanwhile, somewhere in West London, a man in a white Transit van started panicking some time ago.

'It's ten to one,' announces groom Swanley Smith. 'Do you know what time I am getting married at? One o'clock. You know how long it is going to take to get to the church? Half an hour.'

Swanley's van is sitting in a bus lane, not moving. He's waiting for his best man and ushers to catch up. Swanley's going to lead them to the church, even though he doesn't know where it is.

Back at the hotel, Tinie Tempah's 'Pass Out' blares from a car stereo. Josie is in the front garden, gyrating violently to the music, in a world of her own. Extreme stress relief. The flamenco-style front split of Josie's wedding dress is thigh-high. The dress presents her garter to the passing world. Big Chris has given up trying to call the limo company. He's gone down there in person to sort it out.

In another part of West London, Swanley is now leading a convoy of people to the church. Behind him are his brother-in-law, his mum and dad and, in his words, 'some people who are just driving about looking for the wedding'.

Swanley stops to ask for directions to the church three times. Nobody seems able to help him.

'It's now one o'clock,' says Swanley, 'and do you know what time I am meant to be married at? One o'clock. Where are we? God knows. God only knows. We are still about ten minutes away. Ten minutes, half an hour, who knows? If she turns up and I'm not there, she will murder me. The person that is meant to be following us, God knows where they are. I had three following me and now there are only two left.'

At 1.10 p.m., Josie should be already married. Instead, she is sitting on a kitchen chair in the front garden of her hotel, brushing her teeth and dipping the brush in a mug of water. One limo finally turns up. Now they just need the other limo to come, and the bride's Phantom.

Josie's stress levels are soaring. 'Please, God, please let the limousines and the cars pick me up. Please, God, don't let this happen to me.'

Barbara seems to be loving every second of the drama. 'He is probably crying, thinking Josie isn't coming. He'll be thinking, Josie is not coming!'

This sets Josie off. She starts screaming at her mum, who is in turn screaming at Big Chris on the phone.

'The limousines won't come because they all went to the wrong place,' Josie Senior explains. 'We have got one limousine and we have just got your Phantom, which is coming here now.'

Her daughter is losing it. 'We are late already. We have got no time to get there. I think I am about ten minutes late for the wedding already. We are all waiting here and I have no way of getting there. Cinderella can't get to the ball!'

Meanwhile, Swanley finally finds the church. Suddenly, he starts to laugh uncontrollably. Sheer relief?

'Nah,' he says, slapping his knee, 'it is an Indian wedding. It is the wrong fucking wedding. Oh dear me. She is going to kill me stone dead.'

At 1.20 p.m., Swanley and his convoy pull up at another

church. This time, it's the right one. He's relieved that Josie didn't get here first, but the drama is far from over.

At 1.30 p.m., Josie should have been at the altar thirty minutes ago. She's still in Hillingdon. But there's good news: the cars are on their way!

At 1.40 p.m., there's bad news: Josie is stuck in traffic.

At 1.50 p.m., the priest drops a bombshell: he's due in Marlow, on the other side of Henley, at four.

Swanley has told the priest a little white lie. 'I said ten past two; they can't be much later than ten past two. I am a little bit worried because the man there, the priest, is on about if it is any longer, he might not be able to do it.'

At 2 p.m., Swanley is no longer cracking jokes.

He's on the phone to Josie, unconsciously pulling a flower apart in his hand. He's wired. 'Where are you at? . . . Oh, Josie, Josie, what have you done to me? . . . I don't know, Josie, I am stressing out. Where the fuck are you? . . . You are coming to the motorway now! Jesus Christ! Jesus Christ, Josie!'

It's 2.05 p.m. Swanley has bad news: they have only just reached the A40. It's another twenty minutes at least.

'If you are looking at this, Daddy, you should be ashamed of yourself.'

Bridget Doran's mum emerges from the church in Wolverhampton bursting with pride.

'It was lovely, sad. I wanted to listen to every word. The

ceremony was beautiful. I am glad who Bridget married, really pleased for him and her. I cried a lot this morning when I was on me own, but looking at her now, she's happy and she's got a lovely husband – do you know what I mean? – so I hope the two will be happy. And I will always be near her and she'll always be near me because we are very close, me and Bridget.'

Brother Tommy gave her away. Another brother has this message for the man who should have performed that role: 'Tommy is proud of himself because he walked her down the aisle. So we have done our little bit, and if you are look-ing at this, Daddy, you should be ashamed of yourself.'

Bridget may have been brought up by a single traveller mum, but she can't want for anything today. She has the big fat dress, a battalion of bridesmaids, rap-star transport and, waiting at her reception, a fifty-kilo, twelve-foot cake complete with an iced Barbie and Ken. As churlish as it might seem, we ask the bride how her single mum can afford such extravagance.

'Me grandfather put money away for me and me sisters' weddings,' she explains, 'because he wanted me to have a good wedding, because, like, we had no father then to pay for it, and that was his worry, big worry. So he put the money away.'

Later on, outside the reception, a niece pays tribute to Bridget Senior. The teenage girl sums up the feelings of many: 'This is my auntie Bridget and she left her husband when her baby was five months and he is now nearly thir-teen. She planned this wedding all by herself – no man, no help, independent for herself. Her children never wanted for nothing, never needed for nothing. An Irish travelling man and woman could not have done as good for their children as she has. And fair play to you, because you did very good. More than good.'

The girl seals the sentiment by planting a heartfelt smacker on her aunt's cheek. Bridget Senior is overwhelmed by the goodwill and love. 'I am very proud. Very emotional but very proud. Yeah, I really am.'

For Bridget Senior, who is seriously debilitated by arthritis, life without her eldest girl is sinking in. 'She's a lovely daughter. She does everything for me really. She makes me food. She helps me wash me hair. Everything really. I need help with me clothing, she does that. If you're feeling down, she'll cheer you up. She always does make you smile, make you laugh. Thomas is a lucky man, he really is. He must have the four-leaf clover on his shoulder.'

Bridget Junior describes why she will miss her mum so badly. 'I look up to me mum; I don't look up to anyone else. She's always been there for us. Like, with no father there, there's no one else to get really close to.'

As the evening wears on, more and more people turn up. Bridget Senior watches the door like a hawk. If her ex-husband shows, the entire day will be ruined for all.

> 'I look up to me mum; I don't look up to anyone else. She's always been there for us. Like, with no father there, there's no one else to get really close to.'

Meanwhile, at Manchester Airport, a pilot supposedly booked to fly Cindy's groom, Johnny, to the wedding knows nothing about it. He had expected to get all the information through about the flight last night, via email, but it still hasn't arrived. No one's been in touch. He assumes the booking's cancelled. He's not planning to hang around.

Somewhere nearby, Johnny and his panic-stricken party are desperately trying to find the helicopter office. They've been told the flight's booked for a 2.15 p.m. Finally, at 2 p.m., they find what they've been looking for, only to discover there's no booking.

'Just as we got here, the pilot was walking out the door on his way off home,' best man Jimmy pants. 'He never got the details, so he assumed it wasn't happening, which is fair enough. We were told not to come here until quarter past two. We got here dead on two o'clock, thank God, because he was literally walking out the door. Another minute and we would have missed him. We'd be ringing Cindy now, telling her the bad news.'

Fifteen minutes later, Johnny and the boys touch down at the country estate, bang on time.

The groom looks shaken – could be the flight, could be the fact he nearly missed his own wedding. Back on terra firma, all he says is, 'Frightening. It was life-changing.'

Soon Cindy's carriage trots round the corner. The sun shines. Spirit, the owl, doesn't fly off or crash. Three thousand guests don't crash the reception. A shattered Gaynor slips away early, one happy planner.

'Everything went to plan, even the weather. I loved it,' she says. 'The atmosphere was totally peaceful. You get a lot of negative feedback about travellers, but I didn't find any of that. I thought the people were all lovely.'

However, at this unique Christian traveller bash, the free bar has only just opened.

> 'You bleed, we bleed. We are looked at as if we are dirt, but we are not.'

Back in Wiltshire, Bridget Ward and her guests arrive at the baronial golf and bowls club, with Bridget still fearful that as soon as the venue's management realise they're travellers, they will cancel her reception.

When Bridget strolls across the lush bowling green to have her photo taken, she could be any bride. It is when her nine bridesmaids waddle along behind her, all in shocking pink, that the bowlers and golfers get put off their stroke. Suddenly, middle-aged, middle-class women and men stand agog in their pastel linen, staring at the alien pageant.

Bridget's guests are trying to help any way they can. As Paddy Doherty explains in hushed tones, 'Watch the way the travellers talk different here for about an hour; everyone will talk different and be very quiet. It's like you got to kiss backside every time. Of course, it's wrong. Having to hide what race you are, to hide that I'm a traveller. It's like an Englishman hiding that he's English – it's an insult to his family, isn't it, and to his country. We have to do it and we're English; I'm born, bred and reared here. I have got five of my kids buried here and we have to hide our identity. Funny old world, isn't it?'

To the enormous relief of Bridget and her family, the venue doesn't order her to leave or call the police.

Almost as relieved is her best pal and best woman, the irrepressible Elizabeth Doran. 'Well, she was very worried about her venue cancelling and obviously we got here and the people was very, very nice and that was it. Everything's just gone well so far. It is just a release off her. It is like a pressure off her brain with things going so well and everything turning out right. That is good for her.'

The travellers relax and start to enjoy themselves, but Paddy Doherty remains indignant. 'Now look at this place here,' he says, agitated. 'It's out in the middle of nowhere, and we've got to be grateful that we got a place. Look, we're being hidden from society, aren't we? You can be hung, drawn and quartered out here and there's no one here that's going to find you. And this is terrible that you got to look for a function and kiss their arse big time to make sure you get in here. Because we are classed as rubbish. It is terrible to say that word, isn't it? We are not rubbish. We are human beings. We are as good as what you are, you know? You bleed, we bleed. We are looked at as if we are dirt, but we are not.'

Paddy is a proud uncle today. He admires Bridget for putting her wedding off so that Elizabeth could grieve her late father and still be best woman. Paddy pays Bridget his own inimitable tribute. 'She's a very, very honourable young girl,' says Paddy. 'She's very, very polite, very good manners. If you ever stay in her place, she'd get up early in the morning, do you a tea and a sandwich. You know what I mean? She deserves a good partner, a good husband.'

Later in the evening, Bridget has arranged to have a special wedding dance with her best friend, Elizabeth. By then, she will have told her the shock news – that she and Paddy are moving a lot further away than London.

> 'That happy and over the moon, it was unbeliev-able. I realised you were such a beautiful girl.'

In Ivor, Berkshire, Josie McFadden finally turns up for her 1 p.m. wedding, at 2.20 p.m.

An emotion-sapped Swanley just mutters, 'And about time too,' to his flustered bride. The shake of Big Chris's head says, 'Don't even ask . . .'

Josie sat for ninety minutes fearing that she'd miss her own wedding. Now here, she's a burst dam of relief. 'It is really happening now. Yeah, I am really excited. It feels very weird. I will still be me, but I will be married,' she says, before emitting a nervous scream.

The priest, on the verge of calling it off, has to be quick. Swanley's mum couldn't agree more. 'I want it to be over. I want to go home. I am too nervous. I said I was too nervous. I thought my daughter's wedding was bad enough, but this one is worse.'

As Swanley kneels for the ceremony, the handwritten words 'Help me!' are clearly visible on the soles of his shoes. Drunk on relief, Josie gets the giggles.

It seems only minutes later when Mr and Mrs Smith emerge. Josie remains giddy. 'It still hasn't kicked in yet. My name is Josie Smith. I couldn't even look at Swanley because I was so embarrassed. Because I was getting married, I couldn't even look at him straight without laughing and then I had a laughing fit up the aisle.'

For Swanley, the moment was magic. The big man finally shows his softer side. 'When I looked behind me and she was walking up the aisle, I was absolutely stunned. I didn't know what to say, I was that gone for words. I was that happy and over the moon, it was unbelievable. I realised you were such a beautiful girl.'

'There wasn't a dry eye in the house, really emotional.'

At Bridget Ward's wedding reception, one woman is keeping a close eye on the bride's best friend Elizabeth Doran. Thelma has known Elizabeth since she was little. Everyone's just learned that the newlyweds, Bridget and Patrick, aren't moving to London after all; they're emigrating to Canada. Thelma is worried how nineteen-year-old Elizabeth will cope with yet another knockout emotional blow. Less than a year ago, her dad, Larry, died.

'I think Elizabeth will smile all day today,' says Thelma. 'I think that she will probably have a little breakdown, but she won't let anyone see that. She is that type. She's very bubbly. She is infectious. Sometimes you wonder if she is masking her emotions, not only losing her best friend and cousin but thinking about her dad as well.'

Later, the bride and the best woman have their farewell wedding dance. Once again, Thelma is watching closely from the side. 'You could just see how close they are,' she says. 'You know that they are going to miss each other. They were singing to each other, and they were holding on to each other, and there wasn't a dry eye in the house, really emotional. No one interfered; they just let them get on with it.'

> It's a hundred per cent that grabbing is going to be happening tonight at this wedding.'

Meanwhile, Josie McFadden's wedding reception is at full throttle. Among the scantily clad throngs on the dance floor, two fifteen-year-olds are dressed to thrill. Best friends, cousins and English gypsies Cheyenne and Montana Pidgley insist that they are too young to have a boyfriend. However, with dance moves that would trigger a riot in an ordinary nightclub, both are clearly determined to catch the eye of watching boys.

'I think what a travelling boy looks for in a girl is their looks,' says slim, blonde Cheyenne. 'Every travelling girl likes to look their best and to try and look like they stand out, so that when they walk through the door, they go, "Wow!" You know?'

The girls want to grab the boys' attention, but neither wants to be grabbed by a boy – forcibly hauled outside for a kiss.

'No, it is not really my sort of thing. You are trying to go out for a dance, not be trapped in one corner,' says Cheyenne.

Both adhere to a rigid anti-grab game plan. 'Don't go outside. Just stay with the girls and stay where someone is always near you,' says Cheyenne, 'and if you think that someone is going to grab you, just stay out of the way and try and avoid it really. Walk away and be very ignorant.'

If grabbed, their next weapon is to lie. Cheyenne again: 'You make up a lie, like your dad is here or something. That should do the trick. It's a hundred per cent that grabbing is going to be happening tonight at this wedding. There definitely will be grabs here.'

> 'It was a Christian wedding at first, dry till seven, and then it turned into a traveller wedding. All free drink.'

Unbeknown to anyone, Cindy McDonagh's extravagant P. Diddy do, at a country estate in Cheshire, is about to end prematurely.

Sixteen-year-old cousins Martin Tom Doherty and Tommy Sharp, or Mush, are on the prowl. As Mush puts it, 'Martin Tom is enjoying himself, grabbing women. Same as myself.'

In fact, Mush is having a ball. 'The wedding is going nice. Perfect. Everyone is either dancing or singing. It was a Christian wedding at first, dry till seven, and then it turned into a traveller wedding. All free drink. It is nice. It is the way a traveller wedding should be. No fighting, nothing at all.'

As if on cue, a brawl breaks out behind him. Shouting. A woman's screams. Rumbling feet on tarmac. Breaking glass.

Mush doesn't bat an eyelid. 'Travellers have a few drinks, they have a fight. Tomorrow, if they want to sort it out, then fair go and forget about it. That's how it gets sorted out.'

Mush denies that travellers are more violent than settled people. 'It's not about being violent. If a man says something wrong to you, and you don't say something back to him, then you're an idiot. Travelling men, when they get a few drinks down them, they try and, like, be better than you. If you don't answer them back, then you're, like, a waste of space. If you can't fight them back, then you're not a man here. If you fight, then you're a man. If you lose, then you're still a man for fighting him. That's how it is, in our lives anyways.

'If you're a travelling man, you have to stick up for yourself. That's how travelling people is. We got our name; our name is our lives. It's like my name is Tommy Sharp – it's my life.'

By the time police and ambulance turn up, the fight – like the party – is long over. Chief brawlers have scarpered. Everyone is leaving. No one says anything to the authorities.

'That wedding tonight was unbelievable,' says Mush, 'like the helicopter and all the free food and all the free drinks. A very, very good wedding and then afterwards a few arguments. It really got ruined. What can you do?'

Bridget Doran Senior's biggest fear is that her violent ex-husband – and the father of the bride – will turn up uninvited to the reception. She feels his very appearance could lead to trouble.

He doesn't show.

The night – almost over – is trouble-free; the Bridgets are relieved.

'It's gone lovely,' says Bridget Senior. 'Gone nice all day. No arguments or nothing like that. So thank God it's going well and it's nearly over now anyway. I'm tired. Just feeling a little lonely now, knowing she's not coming home tonight with me.'

> 'He informed me . . . that something is going to kick off.'

Meanwhile, at Bridget Rooney's tropical wedding in Lincolnshire, storm clouds are gathering. The hotel is facing its first big test of the day. They had no idea how many people would come. They've laid on a buffet for 150, catering to every possible taste – lasagne, curry, beef, pork, turkey, potatoes, chips, rice and veg – but it looks like far more have turned up. The big worry for deputy manager Will: is there enough food to go round? To run out is unthinkable . . .

As the last knot of guests sit down with full plates, Will breathes again. 'The food is my thing, my issue,' he says. 'Fingers have stopped quaking now. Everything's going fine, absolutely fine. I spoke to the top table. Bridget and

Patrick are over the moon, and the mum, Mary Rooney, is happy, so I can relax a little.'

However, as the evening party kicks off, so do the first signs of trouble. The father of the bride has advised Will to place his staff on alert. It seems that a fight's about to happen.

'He's come over to myself and asked for a word in private,' says Will. 'He informed me, because he says he has respect for my staff and myself, that something is going to kick off. He doesn't know when, he doesn't know how. He says he'll do his best to calm it down. So I'm just logging it with the staff and just seeing if anyone can be in the area just in case. He gave me this information about ten minutes ago.'

The air is filled with eerie menace . . . imminent tropical thunder. Will is tense, stiff, unblinking. He says Bridget's family are trying to stop the fight before it starts.

'All cutlery has been removed from the room,' he says. 'There is literally only plastic and obviously the furniture in the room. Can someone get in touch with the sergeant?'

So far Will has seen only petty squabbles. 'There have been some younger children, about fifteen, that had a scuffle, but that's been resolved quite easily. I've just been told there is another one, but they are resolving that too. No need for a police presence on that one.'

Will's staff are unfazed. Almost.

One says, 'We're not really worried. If something does kick off, it'll be among themselves. I hope. At the moment, we are just taking away the candles, because there are problems with the kids and they have spikes on the end. Just clearing all the tables so everything is ready if it does kick off.'

Meanwhile, Mandy is on the phone to the police. The bride's dad says there will be some problems. You can feel the atmosphere. He says it is going to start at some point and make sure you get your staff out the building.'

Deputy manager Will is put on the line. He repeats what Bridget's dad told him, then confirms that the mood's turned ugly. 'There is an atmosphere in there, but we are trying to keep it normal and see how it goes. The bride's dad says literally be prepared. We are not standing in anyone's way. Literally just get the staff out, close the doors behind us and that is it,' Will says.

Later, Will speaks with the bride's mother, Mary Rooney. She assures Will that the troublemakers are gone. Will warns her that he's keeping an eye on the situation. 'Because we don't want police here, Mary, and we won't think twice.'

Mary reassures him. 'No, they're gone. They've already been removed.'

The travellers have policed their own event. The flashpoint has been doused. Will's confidence is back, and so is the cutlery. He and his staff start the second serving of food.

'She has been dying to get grabbed all night.'

Meanwhile, at Josie McFadden's reception, a girl has been grabbed and hauled outside. It's fifteen-year-old Cheyenne Pidgley, the blonde from West London who doesn't believe in grabs. We catch up with her mid-grab and cornered in the car park.

'Jon, I think it was time you let go of me, don't you?' she calmly tells her grabber. He's not letting her go.

'No. She has already given me a kiss, by the way. I am just chatting to her.'

Cheyenne – realising her good name is on the line – vigorously denies his claim. 'Don't say that. That is a lie,' she says. 'Why are you lying?'

The claim and counterclaim goes on and on. Occasionally, Cheyenne wriggles to get away. It's no good. Jon, who is about sixteen, has her where he wants her.

He explains his technique. 'You get a no for about ten minutes,' he says, 'and then she kind of loosens up a bit and gives you a kiss. Do you know what I mean?'

Again, he raises an arm to prevent Cheyenne's escape. Cool as a breeze, Jon explains his conviction that grabbing is, in fact, consensual. 'The girls are looking to get grabbed, basically. Like this one here, she won't leave me alone. She has been dying to get grabbed all night. It is not my fault. There is nothing I can do about it. Am I right, though?'

Cheyenne is not yielding. 'Please. I think he has had too much to drink.'

Nearby, Montana has been trying to reason with Jon to let Cheyenne go. Now she's giving up. 'Right, I am going . . . I can't be bothered.' As she walks back into the reception, a girl's scream rings out in the night. It may have been Cheyenne.

Jon returns, quietly triumphant. 'I seen her and she was

actually kind of nice, so I thought I would grab her. Luckily, I got a kiss, though, so it is all good.'

Jon's mate, a little the worse for drink, explains how he views grabbing. 'You grab her by the fringe and if she doesn't give you a kiss, crack, crack, crack, crack.'

However, Cheyenne's Romeo denies this. 'There is no hitting involved. You just grab them by the waist and ask them for a kiss and walk them away, basically. Nine time out of ten you get one, but the odd time, you have to drag it out for an hour or two.'

Jon insists that the girls are co-conspirators in the grabbing custom. 'Some girls like to get grabbed because they can't give a boy that they like a kiss until they get grabbed. Do you know what I mean? A girl has to get grabbed before she can kiss the boy. So that is why you sometimes get an easy grab.'

Cheyenne had danced with Jon earlier. 'He is a very good-looking boy,' she says, 'but I don't know him well enough, and if he's decent, he won't be going round saying he got a kiss off me, 'cos he didn't.'

> 'There is no hitting involved. You just grab them by the waist and ask them for a kiss and walk them away, basically.'

In Kent, Lizzie Lee is marrying Johnny – yet another groom who has asked not to be identified. The majority of leading men in *Big Fat Gypsy Weddings* remain anonymous.

One who hasn't is ex-bareknuckle fighter Paddy Doherty, who seems to pop up at most traveller events. Paddy can explain why so many traveller men hide their identity. 'Because they're worried about their living going out the window! If a gypsy knocked on your door and he said he wanted to do some work for you, would you employ him? Truth, would you? No, you wouldn't! Not in a hundred year would you let him do work. Like the groom today. If he does gardening or patching up, cementing, painting, jet-washing, tree-topping, he can't show his face, 'cos people will find out he's a traveller and won't employ him. And yet he's doing nothing wrong. It's all legal, but yet he can't show his face. Why? Because he's a gypsy.'

Big Fat Gypsy Weddings pixilates the face of anyone who requests it. According to Paddy, this will have gorger readers jumping to all sorts of ill-founded conclusions. 'Now, to make matters worse, people watching will think it's 'cos they have something to hide, 'cos they're up to naughty stuff. It's nothing of the sort.'

Lizzie Lee's wedding is textbook wealthy traveller – big dresses, big cake, big car, bar.

Paddy's not surprised. 'Every traveller wedding is better than the last one. It is a competition the whole time. Honest to God, it is a competition. Who dresses the best, whose bridesmaids look the best. A wedding puts a hallmark on what your status is. You get a lot of well-to-do people and they use it to set their status, announce they are what they are, because they know it is going to be the bee's knees. Everything is showing off now. Everything is, "Look at me, look at my children." It is a competition now, isn't it? Sad, isn't it?'

'It's part of gypsy life, a bit of a set-to like that.'

In a classic British countryside churchyard, no-nonsense Romany gypsy Violet Anne Stubley's feeling the pressure.

'Very stressed,' she barks. 'People not turning up on time, but that's gypsies' ways. Nothing ever gets done properly or anything right. Something always goes wrong.'

Violet Anne looks amazing. Her curly hair, eyes and skin all glisten brown against her dazzling yet refreshingly simple white dress. But the bride's in no mood for small talk. Asked how she'll feel walking down the aisle today, she snaps, 'I don't know 'cos I've never done it before.'

The athletic twenty-two-year-old moans about being hot, and about the flies landing on her dress.

Her dad, Bill, and wife, Joan, have lots of practical marriage advice for their blunt, straight-talking youngest. It's easy to see where she gets it from.

'My advice to Violet Anne is to try to keep her mouth shut, because she has got a lot to say,' says Joan. 'I hope it's going to work with Violet Anne because Larry's a quiet lad and he ain't out for a fight. He just wants to go to work, come home. Violet Anne's going to be a bit of a hard case. I think she's going to have a lot of telling off from me. I shall be on Violet Anne's case a bit.'

'Oh, I'll be taking Larry's side,' says bearded Bill.

What can Violet Anne expect if she returns home unhappy with her marriage? 'If she comes back, she's going to be kicked straight back to where she's come from,' declares Joan.

Later, at the Leicester Racecourse reception, Bill declares that the going is good. And getting better.

'I'm only an ordinary lad and I know millionaires, and I've been to their dos and they haven't put better dos on than this, so I'm as good as them in one way. I'm over the moon about it! I've had a right good old do.'

When a scuffle erupts, Bill laughs it off. 'Young fellas do be wild. Part of gypsy life, a few drinks, good dancing and singing and yelping and hollering and a scuffle and everybody loves it, as long as it's not too serious. It's part of gypsy life, a bit of a set-to like that, but only young fellas. They're putting us on plastic glasses, but that's not a problem – we can drink it out of a shoe.

'We're still cooking with gas anyway and a very good day. Hopefully, everybody's enjoyed it. If not, they must have had the toothache.'

Or, in one case, heartache. It seems that everyone's having a ball except Cinderella.

First, Violet Anne explains her eye-bulging stress levels at the church. 'There was so much going through my mind,' she says. 'Like, What am I doing here? Am I doing the right thing? Am I doing the wrong thing? What am I doing? And the heat that was in the church, it was so stressful. It was just, like, Hurry up, quick, get it over with, I just want to get out, and it was just very stressful.'

The ring on her finger doesn't imbue her with any

renewed conviction. 'Hopefully, I have done the right thing, but there is no guarantee on anything. I think we will make it because at the minute we are getting on.'

As the party winds down, Violet Anne fills with dread. Tomorrow, she leaves home. She can't bear the prospect. 'I'm not even going to say goodbye to my mum,' she says. 'It'll be too hard.'

Post-wedding, Violet Anne will swap rural Leicestershire for industrial Slough, her four-bedroom home for a two-berth trailer.

'I've got my own bedroom, my own shower and stuff. From that to a trailer, it'll be tough, but there are lots of pluses. It's much more sociable. And I'll be living with the person I've wanted to live with.'

> 'Hopefully, I have done the right thing, but there is no guarantee on anything. I think we will make it because at the minute we are getting on.'

At the Grove Social Club in St Helen's, it's gypsies on one side of the dance floor, non-gypsies on the other.

Sam, seventeen, has already stopped traffic – literally – with her fourteen-stone pink wedding dress, complete with twenty-one underskirts and fluttering butterflies. Now, as the guests stand confused in the dark, it's time for Sam's pièce de résistance: her lighting-up firefly dress.

Thelma's sewn fifty little battery packs into Sam's dress,

one for each LED and butterfly, but she's not at all sure it's safe. 'Hope so – it does say on the packet they're safe, but you just never know, do you? Look at Michael Jackson. He had everyone looking after him. Anything can go on fire, can't it? So you've got to be very careful.'

Sam replies, 'They were fireworks, not a dress like this.'

'Well, this could turn into fireworks,' snaps Thelma.

'Make sure every light is off,' orders Sam as she enters her reception, her dress aglow, the fake butterflies a-flapping. Thelma's right behind her, fire extinguisher at the ready.

The cheers ring out and damp-eyed Pat Skye Lee is overcome. 'I feel like I am literally the luckiest man in the world,' he says. 'I couldn't ask for a better wife than her. She is everything I've ever dreamed of. All my dreams have been answered.'

Later, Pat is genuinely excited to report that gypsies and non-gypsies are mingling happily.

'Wouldn't it be great if this is how we could always be,' says Pat, 'just living together without judging each other and getting on with it?'

CHAPTER NINE

Post-Wedding Blues

*'It's just once in a lifetime that you can get
someone like her that you can truly trust.
It just can't be replaced. Never.'*

In Trowbridge, Wiltshire, it's the day after Bridget Ward's wedding to Patrick. In a few days, the newlyweds will emigrate to Canada. Left behind in Wiltshire is her lifelong best friend, Elizabeth Doran. Today, the best woman is back in black, out of respect for her dad, Larry.

Elizabeth explains that after a death in the family, immediate relatives don't attend any social events for at least three months and wear black for an entire year. 'It's nothing to do with religion,' she says. 'It's the last thing you can do, isn't it? Like, for your father, out of respect.'

In two weeks' time, the twelve-month anniversary of Larry's death will be marked by the erection of his headstone and the blessing of his grave. The day after that, members of his family will come out of mourning black, but not Elizabeth.

'Because I came out of black for one day for Bridget's wedding, when all me family comes out of black, I'll stay in it for an extra day to make up for yesterday. I wouldn't even have thought of coming out of black and just going into bright pink except for Bridget's big day.'

Getting out of her lurid pink bridesmaid's frock also comes as something of a relief. It's not just traveller wedding dresses that leave scars. 'It's very painful – me hips, me waist. I still feel like I have the dress on! I've got all red marks. When I finally took the dress off, it was like I could still feel the weight.'

However, it's the emotional scars from yesterday that will linger. Throughout her wedding dances with her dad and mum, Bridget cried her eyes out. Then came her farewell dance with her best friend.

'I felt all emotional. But when she was dancing with me and when she hugged me, she whispered in me ear, "Don't cry, like. Don't cry." Then she whispered, "I love you from the bottom of my heart and you're my best friend."'

When she awoke in her trailer this morning, Elizabeth got a surprise. 'I woke up and Bridget was there in the trailer,' she says. 'I was surprised to see her. I asked her, like, why did you come back? She said she had to come back to say goodbye properly to everyone.'

Bridget promises she'll ring every day from Canada. She urges Elizabeth to make some new friends.

'She said to me, "Just ring around the girls and get close

to someone." I just kept looking at her and she said, "Yeah, but you're not gonna do that, are you?" She knows that can't happen. It's just once in a lifetime that you can get someone like her that you can truly trust. It just can't be replaced. Never.'

Elizabeth fears that marriage will change her friend. 'When you get married, you're like a completely different person and you don't even have time for your friends. Girls do change, I've seen it, and she'll have to start doing things his way.

'But Bridgie often said, "I'll never change. I won't change for nobody." So far so good. This morning, she's still the same girl, but I hope she stays like that.'

Having lived such sheltered and controlled lives under their parents' roofs, married life must seem liberating for a young traveller bride. As long as she is with her husband or a relative, she can pretty much go anywhere, anytime. For the first time in her life, she hasn't got kids to mind and other people's mess to clean up. Will the girls relish their newfound freedom for the next few years?

No, says dressmaker Thelma Madine, who keeps in touch with dozens of brides. She says, 'Doesn't matter if they're only sixteen. Being a mother, that's the next thing they want to do. They want to have a baby right away, and if they don't, they are devastated. They think something's wrong with them. They're told, "You have a child right away."'

Of course, every traveller couple is different. For instance,

Josie McFadden and husband Swanley seem to have radically different ideas about planning a family.

Talking alone at a visit to her parents' home, Josie reveals, 'Well, I am not going to plan it, but I am not going to prevent it from happening either. So if it happens, it happens.'

When asked if that means she's not using contraception, Josie slams the lid down on the conversation. 'It is just not clean in travellers' eyes to talk about that sort of thing. It is disrespectful.'

Feeding his horses over at Caterham, Swanley has more specific plans about kids. 'My personal opinion is that I want to leave it about three years before we have a child. I am not going to start a family straight away, because as soon as you have a child, that is when your life really changes.'

Josie's dreams of living near her family in West London are in tatters. She spent weeks hunting for a flat to rent. Mysteriously, every time she viewed a property it would suddenly come off the market. Landlords, it seems, don't want to rent to travellers.

She and Swanley had one other option – moving into a trailer on a piece of land his family owns in Kent, a hundred miles away from Josie's mum and dad. Josie, too young to drive, couldn't stand the idea of being so isolated from her family, so Swanley moved heaven and earth for his new bride – literally.

He created a pitch for them at his family's caravan site. 'The site is technically full,' he says, 'but I got an earthmover and created an extra patch for us. Well, they're closing the site down anyway, so I don't see the problem. It's a pretty good option for us right now.'

Swanley is a relieved man. 'I was dreading the thought of a house. This is far better all round.'

> 'I'll treat her good and everything, but she'll be like my human doll.'

A few months later, we catch up with Josie and Swanley in a café near their new home. They have been married for three months but talk about how dramatically their lives have changed over the past year .

Josie starts, 'This time last Christmas, I was at home, single – no boyfriend, no fiancé – waiting for Christmas with Mummy and Daddy. Now I'm married to him. What's even more weird is that we got engaged in April and then April coming, we'll have our little girl.' Josie is pregnant. Already.

'Until I actually saw the three-month scan, it didn't sink in. I know it sounds stupid, but the thing I'm looking forward to most is I know I can dress her up. She'll be like my little doll, but my real one.'

Swanley looks alarmed. 'It's a human baby!'

'Yeah, I know, but she'll be like my doll,' says Josie. 'I know she's human. I'll treat her good and everything, but she'll be like my human doll.'

Of course, Josie is unfazed by the prospect. She's been bred to breed. 'What's scary about it?' she says. 'I can't really imagine nothing to be scared of. I'm used to looking after kids 'cos I've got my brothers and sisters of my own. Travelling girls are brought up to know what to do with children and how to mind them. I'm going to know what to do. I hope I've loads more children and we're all very happy. We're going to go to our own children's weddings.'

'I cried and giggled and cried and laughed and then cried again all day. I don't know what was going on with me. It's mad.'

The morning after Lizzie Lee's wedding finds her thirteen-year-old sister, Margaret, wrestling with the enormous bridal gown outside the family trailer. Margaret's losing battle to bag up the dress seems symbolic. Now that Lizzie's gone, she's the Cinderella-in-chief, charged with taking care of kids and trailer. It's no wonder the baby-faced brunette spent much of yesterday in tears.

'I'm a bit upset,' she says. 'It's gonna be no Lizzie; it's gonna be me and Mummy! So it's gonna be a bit hard working with Mummy, 'cos if you do one thing wrong, she argues with you. I've got loads to do – clean the trailer and do some washing, packing the wedding dress away, to put it up in the shed . . .'

Today is the day Lizzie, Johnny and the Vivaldi pull off the site in Caterham, Surrey, and move to Watford, on the far side of London. Now, it seems, Lizzie has had a change of heart.

Margaret explains, 'Daddy was crying and he was upset

for her to leave, so I think she's gonna stay here a couple of weeks, till Daddy gets used to her being married.'

A day later, there's been a dramatic fresh twist in the 'Where will Lizzie Lee live?' saga. Now Lizzie's mum, dad and kids have left the site – in the Bordeaux trailer.

While cleaning her Vivaldi, Lizzie explains what's been going on. 'They've pulled to Maidstone, near Kent. All the hassle of the wedding and that, they just wanted to go away and have a break. Daddy's got family there.

'I don't know how to explain it,' Lizzie sighs, exasperated. 'One minute I was cleaning the trailer and the next minute Mummy says, "We're going! Give us a kiss." Then they were all gone. They're mad, they really are; the man and woman's not well! They're not well. Truthfully, I don't know why they went.'

When her new husband, Johnny, gets back from work, the newlyweds will pull away to little fanfare and no family farewell. Lizzie's in emotional turmoil. 'I really do miss them. I've never, ever stayed on this site when they're not here. Not ever. It just feels so different. Especially Simey, 'cos I do love him; the child's my life-support machine.

'Putting my wedding pictures in my album there, I cried and giggled and cried and laughed and then cried again all day. I don't know what was going on with me. It's mad.'

> 'I really do miss them. I've never, ever stayed on this site when they're not here. Not ever. It just feels so different.'

In St Helen's, gypsy tree surgeon Pat Skye Lee and his gorger wife, Sam, are shopping for a new trailer. They have just one specific requirement – it mustn't have a toilet.

Pat explains, 'Travellers wouldn't use a toilet inside the trailer. It is considered dirty. It's like you're actually using the toilet in your kitchen really. You just don't do it. We all have sheds or outhouses. We've got like built-in toilets in them with baths and that, so it's really pointless buying a caravan with a toilet inside of it.'

Like most travellers, Pat waxes lyrical about trailer life, the joy of sites. What strikes you is that the very qualities he likes about it, most newlyweds would hate. 'Whichever window you look out there's always someone there,' he says, 'someone doing something. There's always someone to talk to. People come and go as they please. It's just more sociable. People share: food, chores, tools. It's fun!'

Gorger Sam, firebrand brunette with the blazing eyes, does anticipate one problem with trailer dwelling. 'When we've been arguing, I'll want him out, 'cos there's nowhere for us to go to cool down and keep out of each other's faces. There's no storming off up the stairs! I'll be left looking at his mug, so he'll have to go out when we've had a row.'

Pat's looking for a trailer costing between £5,000 and £10,000. He says he can afford it because he's been working hard for nine of his twenty years. Travellers never have mortgages, according to Pat, but they do have to pay rent to live on a site.

Pat says some – particularly those owned by councils – can charge up to £100 rent per week. 'Council sites normally have better sheds and bigger plots, so they can charge you more money. On top of that, I still have to pay gas, electric, water bills, so it's not really much different to living in a house.'

When it comes to any other expense in life, Pat haggles. Haggling is an intrinsic part of traveller life. Most see it as almost a duty. However, his new wife, Sam, hates it.

'I don't mind with, like, a caravan or with a car or something like that,' she says. 'It's just when you go into shops and haggle for clothes, I feel like an idiot stood there.'

Pat explains how he haggled down the price of the clothes on his back. 'These jeans marked up at forty pounds, T-shirt was twenty-five, and I got the two for forty-five. So that's twenty quid I can spend on cigarettes and drink, diesel, things like that. I would say it is a gypsy thing to do that. I'm sure you'll get used to it. I'll have you doing it before long!'

Sam insists she'll never get used to it. 'I'll walk out the shop before I'll get used to it. He always tries to embarrass me. If we go in a shop, he just does everything he can to embarrass me. Like asking where the freebies are.'

When we meet Sam a few months later in their new trailer near St. Helen's, there is news! Tree surgeon Pat is branching out. He's scrapping timber for something more solid.

'He's moved back on to the scrap,' says Sam. 'It's good money, and it's just other people's rubbish really, so you're

Margaretha and her brother John Boy, whose Holy Communion
outfits were inspired by the film, *Coming to America*

Margaretha at her Holy Communion

Children dancing at a party

Above and below: Girls prepare for their first Communion

Paddy Doherty,
ex-bare-knuckle
fighting traveller

Paddy showing his
fighting moves

Paddy with his wife Roseanne. They have been married for 33 years

Sam and Pat – a marriage between a non-gypsy and a gypsy

Noreen working at the cake shop. She is in a minority of
traveller women who go out to work

Jerry watches his home being demolished
in a row over planning permission

The destruction of the Hovefields' site

Gypsies are hugely proud of their culture and its traditions, and have faced a great deal of persecution in recent years

A magnificent traveller wedding cake

doing them a favour by moving it but you're also doing yourself a favour. It's not, like, the best money in the world, but it's not bad. You could go out all day and just earn about seventy pounds, but then you could work in a proper job and then just earn, like, twenty or thirty, so it is better.'

Sam's a straight-talking woman who gets down to brass tacks. She understands why Pat's gone back to scrap. 'They go back to it because you don't go into people's homes. They worry less about you being a gypsy, so Pat don't feel like he's got to hide who he is, or apologise for it, or give guarantees.'

Sam's made a cast-iron decision of her own: she's going back to work. 'I'm not lonely – I wouldn't say lonely – but it's boring,' she says. 'I can't find a job. All I do is get up, go to the job centre, come back home, and that's my life. Wait till Pat finishes work, make his tea for him when he gets home. If we have kids, I'll give up work then and stay at home. I like the way travellers raise their kids at home. I'll be doing the same.'

> 'I can't find a job. All I do is get up, go to the job centre, come back home, and that's my life.'

In Slough, Berkshire, another straight-talking newlywed is miserable. When she got married, twenty-two-year-old Romany Violet Anne Stubley swapped her family home in Leicestershire for a trailer on her in-laws' site, 110 miles away.

After three weeks, she misses home – and her mum and dad. 'I miss home very, very much. I hate being away from home. I didn't think I would, because I used to say, "I can't wait until I am gone. I hate it here," and now I hate it here where I am at now, and I wish that I was back at home. I was always with mum going to the shop maybe, or going off somewhere. We were always together.'

Violet Anne is on the phone to her parents at least three times a day, and she's been back to visit twice. She says they're sorely missing her too.

'My dad never used to ring me, even if he wanted to know where I was or anything. Now every day he is on the phone. At the minute, mum has got all the grandkids there, so they have been keeping her company.'

Violet Anne isn't just homesick; she's sick of her new home. 'I don't like it. I hate it where I am. I can't wait to be gone.'

In a couple of weeks, she and Larry are moving to a different site. She doesn't know where. She doesn't care where, so long as it's away from Slough. As far as she's concerned, 'Come friendly bombs . . .'

'It is so boring and depressing, and people walk past you like you have got a disease, but that is particular travellers. Some of them think they are too good to speak to you. The rest of them are all right, but they are older and I just want to be away. I just want to be with young people.'

Having been brought up in a house, Violet Anne doesn't want to spend the rest of her life in a trailer. She's already dreading the winter. 'When it is cold, that is when I will dread it. At the moment, it is so hot. At night, I sleep with all the windows open.'

She dreams of a home of her own – not on wheels. 'Council sites are not my sort of thing. Everyone is trying to beat everyone else on here and that is not me.'

This site is home to Larry's parents. Violet Anne feels that newlyweds need to move away from both sets of family. 'So if you are away, you get to know each other's ways better and nobody can interfere in your life. You just get on with it.'

Like most traveller and gypsy women on the road, she accepts that where they live is ultimately up to her new husband.

'Yeah, we could pull up nearer my family, but I leave it up to Larry, though, where we go and where we wouldn't go. Because that is the man's job in the end. That isn't a woman's job. Most people know that South is better than the Midlands and North for work, but we are not sure yet where we are going to go. We might go further on down. Our plans at the minute are to go further on down.'

Once they settle somewhere, Violet Anne desperately wants to get a job. From the day her national insurance card came through the letterbox, Violet Anne has worked. To her, money equals freedom.

'I hate not having my own money now. Every time I go to the shop I keep having to ask him, "Have you got a tenner? Have you got this? Have you got that?" I do like my own money because I have been used to my own money all of the time.'

Larry has no objection to Violet Anne getting a job, but that can only happen after they've found somewhere to live.

On the plus side, she's on top of the housekeeping. 'We haven't had a takeaway in three weeks!'

And at least she and Larry are getting on well. 'Good, very good. Both happy and very good, yeah. Just need to move away from Slough and we'll be fine.'

> 'I hate not having my own money now. Every time I go to the shop I keep having to ask him, "Have you got a tenner? Have you got this?"'

In West London, fifteen-year-old Cheyenne Pidgley – the blonde who dresses to impress – has news. Jon McFadden, the boy who grabbed her at Josie's wedding, has been in touch.

'He started ringing my phone,' she says. 'I just got to know him as a friend and he was a very nice boy and obviously I got to know a bit more about him than I did at the wedding! And he did actually start asking me out.'

Out of every traveller wedding, ten more are created, or so they say. Could Cheyenne and Jon be next?

'No, I'm not allowed a boyfriend. No! He could go back to my dad when I'm sixteen and ask him if he's allowed to go out with me. If your dad says yes, then you're allowed to go out with him then.'

Their romance thwarted by youth, are Cheyenne and Jon West London's very own Romeo and Juliet? She's clearly smitten, but Cheyenne has no intention of flouting the unwritten traveller rule that says you can't date a boy till you're sixteen. 'I wouldn't go out with him secretly. I don't think that's right. I've chatted to him on the phone and that is about it. I'm not allowed a boyfriend, so there is nothing I can do . . . Really and truly, it's the best way to be. Strict rules are for our good. I'd rather live by them rules than if they didn't care about me at all!'

So where does this leave her and Jon? 'I speak to him still. He's like my best friend now, you know?'

Cheyenne still doesn't believe in grabbing, but she does believe that a grab can lead to a more permanent relationship. 'Many people have been grabbed and ended up with that person. Getting grabbed can be a one-off thing. That's the bad thing about it; a girl don't like that. But lots of times it ends up something more.

'It could eventually be him. You never know what life might bring,' she says cryptically.

CHAPTER TEN

Married Life:
Behind Closed Doors

'All travellers believe in big families.'

The *BFGW* brides have celebrated their first anniversaries. Most of them live close to their husband's family. At least three of them are already expecting, but what can they expect from their future lives as traveller and gypsy wives and mums?

This chapter explores the reality of married life for traveller women, behind closed doors. Do men really rule the roost, and how do mums ensure that their children carry on their culture's customs and traditions? We've heard all the hopes, dreams and fears of our newlyweds. Now it's time to see how their lives are actually going to play out.

Dressmaker Thelma Madine says that, just like in settled

society, there are good husbands and bad, with most some-where in between. No matter how their husbands behave towards them, Thelma claims that all traveller and gypsy women have one thing in common.

'They are all controlled,' she says. 'They almost always move in with the husband's family, so his people are watching her all the time. Some of them have to account for where they are every hour of the day. They are not allowed to go to the shops on their own. They have to have some-body with them. And they're controlled by the children as well, because if you've got lots of kids, your husband is going to know where you are all the time. The biggest control is money; they don't have their own money because they are not allowed to work, so everything they want or need they have to ask the husband for. So it's basically, "You be good and you'll get money," so it's like going back to being a child.'

This might sound like a form of bonded slavery to people in the settled community, but, as Thelma points out, she's never met a traveller woman who wants it any other way. 'I think a lot of them like that way of life. None of them has ever said they don't. I haven't spoken to any of them that would say, "Oh, I wish he'd let me do this or that." They've got nothing else to worry about really – bills, mortgage or anything like that. All they have got to do is look after the children, look after the home. It's like a safety net for them because they've been completely controlled by their mother and father. It's just a step on from that.'

Thelma sees many plus sides to the traveller woman's quality of life. They and their children are never lonely.

They are never short of childcare. 'You know, it's such a strong community. That is the upside of it. They can have a nice life with everything they want around them. They don't have to venture into the outside world.'

Ex-bareknuckle fighter Paddy Doherty gives his own inimitable insights into the mind of a happily married Irish traveller man. He says the first thing a traveller woman can expect is loads of children. 'You never hear tell of a travelling family with one or two children,' he says. 'Not unless there are certain reasons. But if they've got big hopes, then they go for a big number of children! We believe in big, big families.

'My granny's called Anne Doherty. She's in the Guinness Book of Records for the most grandchildren and great-grandchildren alive on this planet. She's got four great-great-great grandchildren! She's got hundreds of grandchildren. It's nature taking its course, isn't it? If it was left to me wife, she wanted, like, fifteen, sixteen. It just runs in the breed. All travellers believe in big families.'

Paddy says once children arrive, mum and dad's roles are cast in stone. 'We provide the food, the clothes, the cars, the wagons, whatever they may cost. A woman don't have to work – a traveller wouldn't allow his wife to work. It would be disgracing. It would be shaming him. They can shine up the crockery and look after our children. Their work is not as easy as you think. They're not laid back having a little cigarette or a cup of coffee watching the TV – none of that.'

Paddy knows he sounds old-fashioned to settled people, but compared to his father, he says he's virtually a metrosexual. 'I don't think my father knows how to make a cup of tea. Actually, I do. I make tea millions of times. I've made tea for me and me wife and me cousins, but the old race never believed in that. Of course, don't get me wrong, I wouldn't know how to boil an egg. That's sad, isn't it? But I know how to make a cup of tea. You put a tea bag in a cup and that's it. So I'm good for something. Oh, and I know about a toaster. You put the toast in and then it goes, "Ding." That's the only thing I know: tea and toast and a packet of biscuits. Apart from that, I'm good for nothing.'

Paddy says traveller men draw a firm line at certain household chores. They don't push prams, feed babies or change nappies. 'You'll never see that, not in a hundred thousand million years. To do that, you're making a laugh of yourself. It's just an embarrassment.'

Thelma says traveller men set the rules to suit themselves. She likens them to domestic dictators, not all of them benign. 'Everyone says about king and queen of the gypsies. There is no king or queen; each man is like a king in his family and he makes the rules. I would say that it is a hundred per cent man's world.

'The men can get away with murder,' says Thelma. 'In some families, it's not frowned upon for the men to have affairs. It's just accepted if they wanna have an affair. The women tell you that's the life they want, that's the life they want for their kids, but deep down, who knows? Maybe they don't like it, but there is nothing they can do about it. They've just got to conform. They've got to toe the line, haven't they?'

What happens to traveller women who don't toe the line? There is no conclusive evidence about the prevalence of domestic violence within travelling communities. However, a study in Wrexham, cited in a paper by the Equality and Human Rights Commission in 2007, found that 61 per cent of married English gypsy women and 81 per cent of Irish travellers have experienced domestic abuse. A significant number of those women who had reported the abuse suffered more severe and sustained violence than those within mainstream communities.

It is rare for traveller women to call the police. 'You would be seen as a grass and disowned by the whole community,' says Bernie O'Roarke, an outreach and re-settlement worker for domestic violence charity Solas Anois (Comfort Now), based in London.

Thelma has seen the evidence of domestic abuse first-hand. 'A few girls have called us and they've actually been in a women's refuge when it's got too much. Sometimes you can tell they've had a beating, a split lip, a black eye. But they will go back again. They don't get a divorce. Once they're married, that's it, they can't get divorced. We ask the girls if they're gonna go back to them and they're like, "Yeah, of course. He's calmed down now." And that's it. Quite sad really.'

Some victims think the violence is their fault. 'They just think, Well, I must have done something wrong to get that.'

We filmed Thelma's extraordinary exchange with an Irish traveller bride-to-be called Shirley. This is Shirley's take on violence in the home.

'There ain't going to be violence for nothing. You have to be doing something for them to be violent,' she tells a shocked Thelma.

Shirley goes on to explain why it is wrong for the wife to walk out. 'If you are married to somebody and they are into violence or they are on anything that you don't want them to be on, then that is why you are there for them. You are supposed to stand by them and help them. Like if they are sick and they need help, then you will be there to give it. You can't just get up and walk away. You can't take all the good years and then maybe one bad month comes and you get up and walk away saying, "Well, this wasn't supposed to happen." You have to work at it. It's just like a job. If one day your boss has a go at you, you can't just walk out the door.'

Of course, this is just one woman's perspective. However, the rate of divorce among travellers is far lower than in the settled community. Bridget Doran, the woman who divorced her violent husband, says she's aware of several couples who've separated, but she knows of no other divorced traveller women. Paddy Doherty and his wife, Roseanne, explain why it is so rare.

'Travellers work very hard at their marriages,' says Roseanne. 'It's almost like the thought of divorce doesn't even enter their heads.'

'We don't believe in it,' says Paddy. 'We don't like it. Don't like talking about it either. No, don't even want to have that conversation. A traveller takes it straight to heart. The parents do. Takes it more than bad. It's a shameful thing, see. Not for country folk, but for a traveller, it's a very shameful thing. Your son or your daughter was married and they're divorced now. And bad people think bad things.'

Because a divorce heaps so much shame upon the

couple's families, relatives do all they can to stop it happening.

'The mums and dads are like, "Try. Try again. Do your best,"' says Roseanne. 'Even if the boy says, "No, that's finished," or the girl insists it's over, the family would still be saying, "Please just try again, try again." Like the family won't go away. They're in your face all the time, both sides, to get them back together.'

According to Paddy and Roseanne, divorce is so taboo that many permanently separated traveller couples decide not to take this final, legal step. This doesn't cut them any slack. Divorced or separated, you are still treated as married by most in the traveller community. They aren't supposed to get together with anyone else. If a separated or divorced man or woman starts a new romance, he or she is scandalised – ostracised by many, if not all, in their community.

However, Paddy and Roseanne say things are changing – in their eyes, not for the better. 'Now they're younger, it's getting worse. Now they're starting to leave their wives and their husbands,' laments Paddy.

Others see this development in a more positive light. Says Thelma, 'I'd say some of the younger women are sort of waking up and smelling the coffee a bit, you know, where they say, "Hang on, I don't have to put up with this."'

> 'If you are separated or divorced, stay that way. I don't think it's right to marry a second time.'

In Wolverhampton, Irish traveller divorcee Bridget Doran is still trying to get used to life without her best friend, Bridget Junior. 'Next day, I never got out of bed,' she reveals. 'I just cried and cried. It's really sad, really lonely. I think when you're rushing around for a wedding, you don't think about the loneliness until the next day. You realise then your daughter's gone.'

Happily for Bridget, her eldest girl lives just six miles away and comes round almost every day. 'She just rushes around in the house like she's not married, up and down the stairs doing her usual thing,' laughs her mum.

Bridget moved from the family home into a trailer with local Irish traveller Tommy. However, trailer life isn't that big a shock to her. When Bridget Senior fled her violent ex, she and the kids kept on the move in a trailer for years while he tried to track them down.

'She adjusted to it straight away,' reports her mum. 'She's travelled all her life, Bridget, so I think she was pleased to get back into her caravan. She was happy about that.'

She's also happy with a more recent development . . . She's expecting her first baby.

'Yeah, she is expecting. She's really happy. I'm so glad for her, and shopping for a baby, that should be nice. She'll be a great mum and a great wife.'

Now that her kids are starting to leave home, would Bridget Senior consider falling in love again and remarrying, or is it true that in the traveller community divorced couples are scandalised if they remarry?

'All different people believe in different things,' says Bridget, 'but I believe if you are married and you are happy, stay married, but if you are separated or divorced, stay that way. I don't think it's right to marry a second time.'

Bridget Junior tells us that her mum won't even speak to a single man or a widower. We ask her if this is the case.

'No, I wouldn't talk to them, no way. I don't want to meet nobody else. I wouldn't have time to talk to them,' she says.

> 'It's very rare that a divorced man would find himself a good, honest traveller girl.'

We've learned about the perils of divorce for a traveller woman. What does it mean for a traveller man?

Irish traveller Johnny McDonagh, twenty-four, is the older brother of Cindy McDonagh, whose 'Traveller Wedding of the Year' took place in a country-house estate in Cheshire. Dark-haired Johnny is wiser than his years. He is also one of the growing number of divorced travellers.

'I was barely gone nineteen when I got married,' he says. 'I rushed into it, as so many travellers our age do. She was sixteen and we were seeing each other for about eight months. I don't think that's long enough. I believe that in eight months, you can pretend to be someone, you can fool someone. I didn't give the relationship enough time. If I had it over again, I would have waited at least a couple of years.'

Johnny says that traditional, straight-laced traveller ways are unravelling at such a pace that their divorce barely raised an eyebrow. 'It's kind of scandal for travellers, but two or three weeks later, there is someone else to talk about. That's the way it's going now. There's more and more scandal every few weeks and people are just starting not to be bothered.'

While a divorce is no longer twenty-four-carat scandal in traveller currency, divorcees still pay a heavy price for their 'failure'. Under the unwritten rules of traveller romance, Johnny's prospects of remarrying within his community are limited.

'It's not easy to remarry amongst the traveller community,' he says. 'Even though I'm divorced, a lot of people still class me as a married man because I shouldn't be divorced in the first place. But what could I do? The marriage wasn't working out and I didn't see anything good coming from it, so it was a decision that both me and her made together.

'Everyone wants the kind of girl that's low mileage. You want a girl that hasn't had too many boyfriends, hasn't got a wild reputation. Usually for divorced people, it's either remarrying with divorced people or marrying outside the community. It's very rare that a divorced man would find himself a good, honest traveller girl.'

Even so, the traveller world is still a man's world. For reasons he can't justify, Johnny knows that he's got a better chance of remarrying than his ex-wife. 'I think I could remarry a lot quicker than what she could. I can go looking for marriage; she can't. She's got to wait until it comes to her.'

If Johnny finds Ms Right, he's then got to wrestle with a dilemma of biblical proportions. His options – as he sees them – are, new wife or happy afterlife? If you think travellers take a dim view of divorce, Johnny's religion believes that marriage failure merits eternal damnation.

'I'd like to get remarried. I think I could be a good husband. If someone gave me that chance, I do think I could be a good husband and I would love to rear a family, but my religious beliefs go against that. So I have to make a choice really: am I going to be selfish and do what I think is best for me, or am I going to do what God wants me to do? What's His will for me? That's very important to me. I think I'm too much of a coward to go to hell.'

> 'I'd like to get remarried. I think I could be a good husband. If someone gave me that chance, I do think I could be a good husband and I would love to rear a family.'

Marriage doesn't appear to have made meek the *BFGW* brides!

Inside a spotless Vivaldi trailer, Lizzie Lee is receiving marriage advice from her younger sister Susie. Susie, sixteen, who's been married two months longer than Lizzie, tells her, 'Don't let him take you for a fool – no poker and no pubs!'

Lizzie looks bemused. 'No pokers and no pubs?'

Susie repeats the mantra: 'No pokers and no pubs! Don't let him go off having poker games. Don't let him go to the pub every night. Break the trailer up! Take the key and hide it! And then they can't go nowhere. That's a good technique.'

Susie's rallying cry isn't quite *The Female Eunuch*, but it's a step towards marital equality.

'Don't cook every night,' she advises, 'and if he wants to go to the pub, you go with him. Make him take you with him. Men like a night out by themselves in the pub. That's OK, but not all the time. You've got to take as much as you give, so you make him take you out too.'

Susie and Lizzie live in trailers on separate sites, among their husbands' families. 'When you get married, wherever your husband gets work, that's where you go. Every travel-ler girl's the same,' explains Susie.

Neither drives, so they're stuck. As Susie says, 'I live about forty miles from my family, but it feels like hundreds of miles 'cos you can't see them when you want. It is hard, because I never knew anybody on the site when I moved there. And it's silent, dead quiet. You just don't hear no noise at all. And it just makes you sit and think about your family. And then you start missing everyone again.'

However, Lizzie – still in the first flush of newlywed life – seems at home with the peace and freedom. 'On Monday, I just went into town without making the beds or tidying up. It feels great! We'd never be allowed to do that at home.' She smiles at her own mini-revolution. It's hard not to think of poor Margaret, crushed rebel, scrubbing away in deepest Surrey. 'She probably has the odd little cry,' says Lizzie, 'but she'll be OK.'

Lizzie tells Susie she should make the most of the peace and freedom too. While it lasts. Susie, sixteen, is expecting her first baby.

While a mum-to-be is often consumed with anxiety about raising a child, Susie couldn't be less fazed. 'People say the midwife comes out and teaches you how to bath the baby and I already know how to do all that,' she laughs.

'When Simey was born, I moved into my mum and dad's trailer and used to do his night feeds and wash him and everything. I know how to do everything really.'

> 'When you get married, wherever your husband gets work, that's where you go. Every traveller girl's the same.'

In Slough, another *BFGW* bride dishes out more than hot meals to her new husband. When talking about marriage, forthright Romany Violet Anne Stubley could be describing how to break in a stubborn horse: 'Keep your foot down. Have the reins on them. Don't be their dog.'

Violet Anne has seen what happens when a wife lets her husband off the bridle. 'It's a man's world. If you let them run, then they will. Pub every night. Dressed up and off down the town and you will be stuck at home like a divvy. No, that isn't me. I wouldn't be stuck like a divvy. If you let them get away with it, then they will do it.'

How easy is it for a traveller woman to stand up to an errant husband? Even tough-talking Violet Anne knows that, for some wives, complaining is not an option.

'Maybe if those women did try and be strong about it, then maybe they would get beat. Maybe they would get their brains bashed in by some of them psychopaths.'

Violet Anne believes that marriage can't work for anyone expecting it to bring freedom.

'When they're married, they must think, Oh, I want to start going out now and enjoying myself. Then maybe their husbands won't let them or their wives won't let them, so they think, I can't stick this, and they realise that they are grown up and they can do what they want. They don't need each other.'

Violet Anne, twenty-two, has some hard-bitten advice for love-struck teens: 'Do not get married. Wait. Enjoy yourself as much as possible and wait for as long as you can. Get it out of your system while you can and then when you get married, it is time to settle down.'

> 'Maybe if those women did try and be strong about it, then maybe they would get beat. Maybe they would get their brains bashed in by some of them psychopaths.'

About half of all traveller and gypsy families now live in houses. The other half live in caravans, whether on private sites, council sites or unauthorised encampments. Because traveller sites tend to be tucked away and screened by fencing, gorgers never get to see day-to-day life inside. Then Paddy and Roseanne Doherty opened their site to *BFGW*.

Inside Paddy Doherty's flash chalet on the council-owned Duchy Road Traveller Site, wife Roseanne is busy sorting through a pile of mail. Roseanne helps with the mail because most tenants on the site can't read or write. Helping people with their correspondence isn't part of her husband's job description. As Roseanne reveals, not much of what they do here is. On paper, Paddy's job as a site caretaker is to maintain the thirty-one-pitch site and collect rent. In reality, he and Roseanne's pastoral duties include peacemaking, marriage counselling and ejecting troublemakers.

'It's almost sheltered accommodation,' says Roseanne, without a hint of complaint. 'Paddy's always here for any problems that they might have. If there's anything like domestic violence, the women always come over to Paddy. If the police come here, they'll knock here first and Paddy will go over and help them get talking – you know, things like that.'

Roseanne explains why tenants prefer a site run by a fellow traveller. Paddy understands their ways, and crucially, he's here 24/7. What use is a nine-to-five council-jobsworth warden when all the action kicks off at night?

Roseanne again: 'People know that whenever they've got a problem, they can always come here, no matter what time it is, day or night. If there's a domestic in the middle of the night – maybe the husband might be drunk – the women know they can come to our door, it's never locked, and talk to Paddy about it. Sort things out, basically. It's like one big family really.'

Paddy appears to excel as a peace-broker. 'He won't allow bullying whatsoever. Paddy's got a way of talking to people. He's got a way of saying, "Don't do that. Yous are silly," and the women knows they can go to Paddy and he can stop it. Men just have respect for him.'

How does Roseanne like being godmother of Duchy Road?

'If I won the lottery, I still wouldn't want to leave here! I've got the comfort here in the chalet – the comfort of a house – but I've got the company of everyone on the site. I don't think I could live without that! Imagine if I was in a house. I wouldn't see anybody.'

Paddy's outside, repairing a section of Duchy driveway. He's wearing his trademark jeans and white vest. *Die Hard* Doherty.

When it comes to talking about his site, Paddy is almost evangelical. 'I have won the lottery, haven't I?' he says, tattooed chestnut-brown arms outstretched. 'You know the Queen lives in Buckingham Palace and we live here, but I swear on my baby's life this is Buckingham Palace for me! I know you'll say, "Oh, you're a madman." But this site's the most beautiful thing you could ever walk on. Look at it! Is this not the dog's bollocks? Blue sky. Lovely trailers. Lovely homes. This is five star.'

The site is spotless. Paddy even gets Pest Control out every six weeks to exterminate any interlopers. CCTV cameras peer down from all corners, providing another kind of pest control. 'They do my job for me,' says Paddy. A few weeks ago, CCTV picked up a young man on the site stealing car batteries from his grandfather. Paddy showed the old man the video evidence and, with his blessing, evicted the thief. No police, no courts.

'Isn't that a better way all round?' asks Paddy

rhetorically. 'I don't want to get that lad a record and ruin his life. At the same time, justice has to be done.'

The thirty-one plots are taken by English, Irish and Scots traveller families. In all, this is home to over a hundred people. Some have settled here for good. Most will move on, after months or years. 'Moving on is their way of life, isn't it?' says Paddy.

It is Paddy's sole decision who is allowed to stop here and who isn't. And that's why the letters P.D. are painted three feet high in the middle of the road, just before you enter.

'I'll tell you what "P.D." stands for,' says Paddy. 'You're not coming on this site taxing any of my tenants, bullying any of my tenants. That's who I am! P.D. Paddy Doherty. Because there's a lot of travellers on here that could be very easily intimidated. There's a lot of people that would come in here and take their things off them, and it's wrong, isn't it? I won't allow it on here! Honest to God, I won't.

'It is very easy to check travellers out. Name is everything in travellers. If you have got a bad name, then they won't pull on.'

Once you do pull on to Duchy Road, Paddy has a list of site rules.

All kids eleven or under have to go to school: 'It's very important that children get educated. You get a lot of adults that can't read or write. I can barely read. I'm ashamed to say that, but what I missed out on I make sure the other children didn't miss out on.'

Families have to keep their plot clean: 'You'll see no fly-tipping or scrap on this site.'

No bullying or intimidation: 'I'll tell you once, I'll tell you again, I'll tell you three times, but I'm not going round and round the roundabout. After three warnings, it's get off! I'll evict you straight away.'

Paddy reveals his technique for dealing with trouble. 'I'll go and sort it out. In two minutes! Even if it's two o'clock in the morning, I'll run over there. Everyone's got to have a kind of uncle . . . Uncle Paddy! And they have to look up to you – not like you're intimidating or bullying – but they look up to you. They'll stop 'cos it's me. As long as no police gets involved and there's no one get hurt out of it, it's all OK.'

CHAPTER ELEVEN

Something Old, Something New

*'That's where we come from, around
the stick fire ... To think we're talking
about posh weddings and houses and
the like.'*

E very traveller or gypsy dad we meet seems consumed
by a single primary mission in life – to ensure that his kids
preserve his culture's customs and traditions. Traveller and
gypsy fathers see themselves as custodians of their culture.
They talk passionately about bequeathing their way of life
to the next generation, no matter how out of step it may
seem with the modern world.

This generation of traveller parents, however, faces
basic survival pressures. Where are they going to live? In

an increasingly computerised and regulated world, how will they earn a living? For how much longer can they insulate their children from the outside world and its heretic influences?

Most traveller men will go toe to toe with anyone, but they can't fight the march of modern life. The traveller men we spoke to realise with mournful certainty that they are powerless to prevent change. The change they see in their communities they don't like. In unguarded moments, they lament the erosion of traveller values and morals, the loss of ancient traditions. One man's story might help gorger people appreciate just how fundamentally life has changed for Romany and travellers over the past forty years.

If you went in search of mythical Middle England, you'd happily plump for the village of Stanton-under-Bardon in the heart of Leicestershire. With its bustling post office, thatched pub and two well-tended churches, it is quintessentially English. This is home to Bill and Joan Stubley, parents of straight-talking Violet Anne and three other grown-up children. Their four-bedroom brick home – self-built by Bill – couldn't be more at odds with their upbringing. Romany Bill and Joan grew up in trailers. They knocked doors for scrap and rags, and picked fruit for cash.

'That's where we come from, around the stick fire,' says bearded, genial Bill as he looks at photos from his child-hood. 'I mean, look where we come from! To think we're talking about posh weddings and houses and the like.'

Bill remembers endless hot teenage summers picking strawberries in Norfolk. 'On a Saturday night, they'd all be in the dance and the fingers would be red where they'd been working all week for three or four quid just to get down town of a Saturday night, just enjoying themselves. It's not like that now. You don't get gypsies picking fruit or working on farms. We used to knock on doors for groceries or go to the village shop and haggle for a few bits. Me and my missus last night went to Sainsbury's.'

What lay behind Bill's decision – eighteen years ago – to put down roots?

'I wanted to go up the ladder a bit, I suppose. I just wanted to improve my life a little bit. It kept us skint for a long, long time. Bread and jam for four years solid. We ain't got over it yet, to be truthful, but eventually we're getting there.'

Bill and Joan are modern traveller parents. Even before they settled, they ensured that their kids got schooled.

Bill explains why. 'I've never been to school, not for one day, never, ever in my life. I didn't need to go to school years ago, only had to knock on a door and ask them if they got a bit of scrap and rags. Them days are gone, so we need an education even just to survive.'

Bill's eldest boy got bullied at school for being a 'gypo'. His second son put an end to that. 'He called this bully out – *bhooosh* with a house brick on the back of his head, hospitalised him. He had to have stitches and that. That was the end of it; he was never a bully no more.' Bill's ho-hum tone says, 'Fair enough.' It's hard to disagree.

Almost two decades of home ownership in aspiring Stanton-under-Bardon hasn't changed local attitudes. Bill says he's still treated like an alien.

'The first thing out of their mouths is, "It's you lot!" If a bike tyre gets let down in the next county, I've heard them say, "It'll be some of you lot." Gypsies are certainly not perfect, but it's the same in every community. Why should they keep pointing the finger at us all the time?

'If you do have the luck to get a nice car or something like that, you're interrogated. "You don't pay this, you don't pay that!" A load of bull – you've got to pay now-adays. We had to pay our council tax otherwise they'd take the house away off us. We have to pay everything same as everyone else.'

Just last night, Bill had a brush with what he considers a racist barman. 'Abartheid', if you will.

'About half nine last night, we went up for a pint and to get something to eat. There was four adults and two young lads. One's fourteen year old. He's almost as big as me, not little babies. The man come straight over and obviously he can see we're travelling people and he says, "No children in here after ten o'clock."

'Ten o'clock come, he's straight over to us. There are seats outside, lovely night, so we said, "Let's just sit outside." "The children can't sit outside," he says, big old boy as well. We say, "OK, we'll go and sit in the car, in the motor." So he says, "No, they've got to get off the premises." So we just left, brought them home.

'We never raised our voices or anything, because it's only in the village where I live and I wouldn't want to make a scene. But as I was going off, the police car was coming onto the car park. I couldn't understand his point of view really, but that is all part and parcel of being a gypsy.'

It seems there's something about Bill Stubley and publicans . . .

'When the landlord took over, he actually come walking up the drive to introduce himself to me. "You're Mr Stubley," he said. I said, "Yeah, you can see what I am, a gypsy." He said, "I don't mind you coming in for a drink, but I don't want you coming in with your friends." So I was meant to go in and drink on my own. But then I was on my own property, so I told him to turn round and eff off back there before I put a shoe in his arse. I couldn't help it! I thought, Well, you get back there – I don't need you. I've never been in it since, so that was the end of my very local pub.'

Drinking in his local is not the only thing that's come to an end for Bill. He accepts that roaming is over for the Romany. What worries him is how other traditions are dying out with it.

'Nobody wants to come home from work and face a heap of policemen towing you off. Them days have gone and you've got to live with it. A lot of people nowadays don't even talk like travellers. They forgot where they've come from. They're mixing in with the settler people, like gorger people, and after a couple of year they talk like them.

'The Romany tongue is a lovely thing to have, part of our culture. There is actually classes now. Young people are going to classes and learning their own language. These are young travelling people. I've never heard anything like it. Their parents should have taught them. I've used Romany terms to thirteen- and fourteen-year-old gypsies and they hadn't a clue what I was on about. It's unreal, shameful really. If we can't pass on our culture to our own kids, what chance have we got?'

'The Romany tongue is a lovely thing to have, part of our culture. There is actually classes now. Young people are going to classes and learning their own language.'

The travellers and gypsies on *BFGW* seem to revere their kids and their elders. No one had ever heard of a traveller family putting an elderly relative into a care home.

'We mind them,' says our friend Paddy Doherty, site godfather. 'That is our duty to our parents. That is how we have been brought up.'

When a traveller or gypsy dies, family and friends travel from all over the country to attend the funeral. Because travellers tend to have large families, funerals are often major productions. It's uncommon for fewer than a few hundred to show up. Most travellers on *BFGW* say they attend as many funerals in a year as they do weddings – often somewhere between ten and twenty. Perhaps it is this familiarity with death – the constant reminder of their own mortality – that gives travellers their *joie de vivre*. Perhaps this is why they put so much effort into happier occasions. Another reason travellers attend more funerals than gorgers is that they have a lower life expectancy.

Over half of travellers do not reach the age of fifty.

Many of the *BFGW* contributors have had their own

personal tragedies to contend with. Take Paddy and Roseanne Doherty. They've buried five children. Four died in infancy. Their oldest boy, Patrick, was killed in a car accident in 1996, aged eighteen. His two cousins Andrew and Davie also died in the crash. Patrick shares a gravestone with Davie, who was a close friend.

Patrick loved cars, which is why every time his dad gets a new set of wheels, he takes them up to the local cemetery to show to his firstborn.

'I like to do silly things like this. It keeps me happy and I wanna show him my car and discuss it with him,' explains Paddy. 'I made a promise to my Patrick years ago. Anytime I get a new car, I always bring it up to Patrick just to have a look at it. Even if you say, "How can he look at it?" He's dead to other people; he's not dead to me. He loved cars and he loved music and singing. I just show the car to him, play one of his songs on the CD player. When that song has finished, then I'll go on then.'

As Paddy plays one of his son's favourite songs full blast, he tries to explain what losing him felt like. ''Cos he was my firstborn, he's everything. Your firstborn is your legend. You're gonna make him what you never were. You're gonna give him the things you never had. Hair as black as soot. Brains – he was an old man before his time. Everyone loved him because he was so honourable. Wasn't cheeky, wasn't cocky, wasn't arrogant. Everyone loved his presence. When I go to see my Patrick, I just wish to God that I wasn't going to see him in a graveyard.'

Paddy will never forget the day his son died. 'Patrick was with me all that day. We went swimming all that day, me, him, his sister and his brothers. When he left me, he was only gone twenty minutes. I got a phone call saying he was dead. I couldn't believe it. Couldn't be dead, I say. Couldn't be. Inside twenty minutes, he was dead, him and his two cousins, my brother's oldest boy and me cousin's oldest boy. Terrible, terrible tragedy. Me boy, I put everything into him. I do think God was teaching me a lesson for all the bad things that I've done, all the wrong things.'

Needless to say, he and Roseanne have never got over it. 'People thinks your child's dead over a year, you get over it. You don't forget it. You don't. I don't know, sometimes I come here and have a good laugh, good joke. Sometimes I come here and I'm on a downer, like. Honest to God, I've been here, you start crying for nothing at all. Oh, life, honest to God, life is very cruel.'

Every year on the anniversary of Patrick's death, Paddy and his family hold a memorial at his graveside.

'I get drunk every year at his grave, celebrate his life and his cousins who died as well. Play his songs and we have a good laugh. It's a celebration of their lives.'

This year, Paddy allowed us to join in the unorthodox graveside tribute. Dozens are here, swigging beer from cans and bottles, and listening to Patrick's CDs on a car stereo.

Paddy is touched. 'Every single year I've come back and every year there's more people. It gets bigger and bigger – lovely respect.'

Paddy gave his eldest son the nickname Spinks, after heavyweight boxer Leon Spinks, who beat Muhammad Ali. Paddy shows where the name Spinks is inscribed on the headstone. 'Patrick used to love fighting when he was small and I nicknamed him Spinks when he got his two front teeth knocked out and it never left him. And if you look on here, on this heart, you see I call him Spinks there.

'He's a good-looking lad, isn't he?' he says, pointing at Patrick's picture. 'He was a man's man. He was everything a father could ever want. He was more.

'My Roseanne, she don't care who listens and who don't listen to the CDs – she plays them. My Roseanne is very laid-back, but when it comes to Patrick, the whole world could blow up. My poor Roseanne, she never did get over my Patrick. She's still not over him, I don't think.'

Roseanne is speaking directly to Patrick's headstone. 'It's like the genie and the lamp – if I could just have one wish, I wish God spared you. But then that doesn't even give you one little bit of a hint as to how I'm feeling. Fourteen years passed now, but he was mine and I loved him. He was me oldest and the first to do everything and I'm so proud of everything he did. I loved him so much.'

Roseanne is overcome.

Paddy turns to us. 'Now if she gets drunk today, she'll have a good cry, I'll go home with her tonight, and she'll say, "Come on, Paddy, we need to dance," and me and her will be dancing. Honest to God, mark my words, me and her will be dancing tonight in the front room, all night with his CDs on, and then we're like a little boy and girl again, like sixteen-year-olds. Me and her will dance all night.'

The next day, Paddy and Roseanne return to the grave-yard to pay a more personal tribute.

'You see, me and her come back here on our own now and we do this grave once more. She'll spend about two hours here, me wife. Yeah, sit down and she'll do this and she'll do that, but she's happy like that. Do you know what I mean? It's absolutely lovely. I know it's sick saying a graveyard is lovely, but look how quiet and peaceful it is. It's beautiful. All your worries go out of your head.'

Paddy reveals that he's bought all of the plots around Patrick's grave. 'Yeah, I got my grave. Me and Roseanne will be near the benches there. I got me four sons' and me daughter's graves. Sooner or later we are all going to die. No matter who you are or what you are, you can't shirk that. I want my children to be with me when they die.'

It seems, though, that travellers are considered second-class citizens by some even beyond the grave.

Paddy tells us the story. 'You see this grave right here where my Patrick is? There was a man buried there right next to him, God rest his soul, and the dead man's widow used to go to church with my mother every Sunday. And then one traveller got put here, God rest his soul. This woman didn't like the idea of travellers coming here, so she dug her husband up. It took about two years to get permission to get her husband dug up, yeah? Little had she known I would have happily paid for it. I would have paid because I wanted that grave right beside Patrick. She took her husband up and she put her husband next to the toilets right over there. She got her husband put next door to a toilet before she would have him here next to travellers.'

> 'They're going to bring in the big machinery, the big bailiffs, and they're just gonna smash everything and leave us homeless.'

Children are the hub of traveller life. In settled society, kids often have to fit in around the lives of their parents. They are dropped off at childminders', sent young to nurseries, signed up to after-school clubs. Not so in the traveller world. Here, kids come first. Everything revolves around them. The vast majority of traveller and gypsy children are raised at home by their mums.

As Thelma says, 'We can learn a lot from them. How many settled women would love to be at home with the kids instead of trying to juggle it all with their careers? Travellers wouldn't dream of handing over their child to a virtual stranger.'

The only time a young traveller child leaves their site is to be taken to Mass. Most traveller mums we spoke to bring their kids to church every Sunday. The vast majority of Irish travellers are staunch Catholic. As a result, the milestones in a traveller's young life tend to be religious: their christenings and, most extravagant of all, their first Holy Communion. Each ceremony is marked with a big party. Relatives and friends come from all over the country to celebrate.

Of course, this is partly due to the fact that family occasions are the mainstay of traveller social life, but there are other reasons why travellers and gypsies make such a big deal of life's watershed events. The more a minority feels under threat, the harder it clings to its culture and traditions. So much is uncertain about the future of travellers that christenings, Communions and weddings give a sense of continuity and permanence, of longevity and perpetuity. For travellers, life's ceremonial stepping stones are vital for their very survival. Each baptism, Communion and wedding is a passing of the cultural baton to the next generation.

All the traveller brides in *BFGW* spoke about their commitment to keeping their culture going. It is hard-wired into their make-up. 'I will bring up my kids in the same way,' is a comment made by each of the marrying girls, without exception. For parents, occasions like a first Holy Communion are an opportunity to instil this conviction in their own children.

Catholic children usually receive their first Holy Communion aged seven or eight. It is the first time in their young lives that they receive the body of Christ in the form of unleavened bread. For girls, it is the first time in their lives that they get to wear ceremonial white.

Thelma Madine now makes dresses every bit as elaborate and expensive for first Holy Communions as she does for weddings. Pound for pound, these seven- and eight-year-old girls haul as much frock 'n' rock up the aisle as any of our traveller brides.

Some parents see their daughter's first Holy Communion as a dry run for her wedding. It can also be a way of seducing that young girl with the 'princess for a day' wedding fairy-tale.

For some of the little girls in diamond-studded dresses, the message from their parents is crystal clear: if you're a good girl, you can have your dreams made real. A girl's Disney fantasies can come true, so long as she toes the line. Little wonder, then, that from their Communion day forward, most young traveller girls are preoccupied by their wedding day. Perhaps unsurprisingly, it's the mums driving the first Holy Communion express.

'Communion Mum' is often in her early or mid-twenties. She sees her daughter as a living doll, a mini-me. Communion Mum wants her daughter to outshine all others. Maybe that's because Mum's wedding day has since been eclipsed by a sister or a cousin. Maybe it's because she craves the status of outdoing the opposition. Maybe it's because she's starved of attention and kudos in her own life. Or maybe she just really likes bling. No matter what it is that motivates Communion Mum, she is one driven woman.

Thelma has just finished a Communion gown inspired by the Eddie Murphy film *Coming to America*. It's for seven-year-old Margaretha from Stroud in Gloucestershire. She's taking her Communion on the same day as her brother John Boy, who's sporting an outfit from the same film. John Boy will be an African prince for the day, resplendent in dazzling white quasi-military uniform and white winkle-pickers. It's banana republic dictator chic, but austere compared to Margaretha's pink monster meringue. Her dress is made from 500 metres of pink netting, with a corset, a crown and a natty little brolly. Covered in 5,000 crystals, it is more than twice her body weight. She and John Boy are the only traveller kids in their class taking their Communion vows.

The following Sunday, the African prince and princess

are ferried to the church in a white limo, complete with bottles of fake champagne. The other kids watch Margaretha squeezing out of the limo in open-mouthed disbelief. To support the crippling weight, she then has to lurch side to side, zombie style, towards the church. Her classmates can't help but giggle. It's hard to watch their unintentional cruelty.

To avoid such a culture clash, some mums arrange all-traveller Communions. You'd expect the competition here to be white hot. Curiously, there's an unspoken consensus that all the girls should look as tanned, made-up, bridal and glittery as each other.

One all-traveller Communion is taking place near Basildon in Essex. Two of the girls, both named Mary Ann, are aged just six. One of the girl's mums – who, based on looks, can't be older than twenty-four – explains why they're jumping the gun.

'The reason being we're facing eviction here from these yards,' she explains. 'We don't know when it's going to happen – it can happen any day – so now that we have the chance to have this first Holy Communion done today, we're going to do it. 'Cos if we get evicted out of here, we all have to go our separate ways. We won't be all together, you see. So all her friends are around at the minute, so she'll have a nice little party today with her friends.'

These Irish travellers live on Dale Farm, Essex – now Europe's biggest site. Travellers bought the land and began settling here almost a quarter of a century ago. As their families expanded, so has the population. It's now home to about a thousand people.

The site features a number of plush brick chalets that wouldn't look out of place on a swanky private housing estate in nearby Chigwell, *The Only Way Is Essex* capital of bling. But although the Dale Farm occupants own the land, they don't have planning permission to live here.

Margaret again: 'About seven and a half year we've been here, fighting our court case for five year, lost everything, and now they said they just want us out. They're going to bring in the big machinery, the big bailiffs, and they're just gonna smash everything and leave us homeless. They don't want us here 'cos we're travellers.'

Their local council is evicting the travellers on the grounds that they've spilled out over the original farm boundaries. They are now a blot on green-belt land. Yet before it became a traveller site, Dale Farm was an ugly eyesore. The site was a concrete, metal-strewn scrapyard. Besides, campaigners say, if the council is so concerned about preserving green-belt land, why has it sanctioned the construction of luxury private homes just up the road?

In a telling exchange, six-year-old Mary Ann learns about the threat of eviction from an older cousin named Eileen.

'We have to get this letter,' says Eileen. 'It's called a twenty-eight days' notice – by the end of that twenty-eight days, a lot of bulldozers come in and they will dig up all the tarmac and knock down all the walls and then burn down the chalets.'

Mary Ann is aghast. 'I'm shocked,' is all she can say.

Eileen is aware we're watching. 'She only knows about it now,' she tells us. 'She only found out now.'

Mary Ann is still coming to terms with what she's just

heard. 'I hope that don't happen. If it does, like . . . No, if everything burns down, we're going . . .'

Eileen finishes the sentence Mary Ann can't bring herself to finish: 'We'll have to live on the side of the road.'

Mary Ann is a lot older than she was five minutes ago. Of course, Mary Ann and Eileen have no idea that they are not allowed to live by the side of the road any more. There is nowhere left for Mary Ann's family to park. They are being legally corralled into either settled sites or housing, but there aren't enough settled sites. For travellers, Prime Minister David Cameron's Big Society seems to be shrinking all the time.

The thing that annoys campaigners most about the proposed Dale Farm eviction is children's welfare. Travellers are constantly criticised for removing their children from education, yet between ninety and a hundred Dale Farm kids regularly attend local schools. If they're ousted from their homes, the kids can forget about education. They'll spend weeks, maybe months on the road engaged in a relentless game of cat and mouse with police and local courts intent on moving them on. You can't get schooled on the run.

Just a week earlier, bailiffs and earthmovers smashed up the Hovefields Traveller Site, three miles down the road. The travellers here are convinced that Hovefields was a Dale Farm dry run. In Basildon, it seems, The Only Way Is Eviction.

So, this Holy Communion feels like a Last Supper for Dale Farm. Maybe a Last Supper for travellers in limbo on 'illegal' sites.

'This party's very special,' says Margaret, ''cos it's going to be the last party we'll have on Dale Farm. We'll be on the road, I imagine, after this. We might have a party on the side of a motorway next time you see us. In some car park.'

All they can do is live for today. And today is the day before Mary Ann's Communion. Mum Margaret takes the six-year-old for her first ever spray tan. The following morning, the makeover steps up a notch. The Mary Anns will receive Christ for the first time thick with mascara, rouge, eyeshadow and glitter spray.

Later that evening, as the sun sets over Dale Farm, the Communion kids party hard.

'Everyone is enjoying it,' says Margaret. 'No one's talking about getting evicted, because we're having a party. We're ignoring it. We're celebrating today. We're forgetting about what's happening tomorrow and the next day. Today is all about the kids.'

Tomorrow is about taking a stand against the bailiffs – so says Mary Ann's grandma. 'I would die for my grandchildren,' says grandma, 'and if the bailiffs come in here and think that they're just putting us out of here, goodbye, no resistance, they have another think coming. Because they will have a hard fight on their hands. How can you bring children out on the side of the road with no sanitation, no schooling, no doctors' surgeries? And they're always on about children's welfare. Where is the welfare for gypsies and traveller children? There is none.'

The Dale Farm residents – just like the Hovefields travellers before them – have nowhere to go, so they plan to stay. As Margaret explains, 'This is our last stop. If we don't stand up and fight now, well, it's going to keep happening. We're never going to be able to buy a piece of ground that's going to be our own and move onto it, so we're going to have to make a stand somewhere and it's going to be here. We're going to stand and fight this now. There's a lot more people here and there's a lot of us ready to stand and fight because we're just sick of it.'

> 'It is just this big dress. The girls are done up like a little bride.'

Not all Communion Mums want their daughters to leave school early and settle for lives as housewives and mums. Typical of the modern traveller mum is Helen Collins, from Gorton in Manchester.

We meet Helen at Nico, Thelma Madine's emporium of excess, where two of her three children are being fitted for their Communion. Helen, her husband and their kids have sampled life in a trailer and in a house, both in Ireland and in the UK. Now she feels settled in Manchester. She likes the perks of home living – hot water, heating – and her kids are thriving in the local Catholic school. Helen wants all three kids to stay on in education.

'I never had a good education. I was took out of school when I was quite young,' says Helen. 'I would like them to stay right up until they are at least sixteen because there is nothing for them to do in the house. If they were clever enough to even get a few GCSEs and hit college, that's what I would love.'

Helen accepts that life on the road is not practical any

more. One factor is that her kids seem to prefer living in a house. Daughter Katie, seven, has made her mind up. 'The best thing about living in a house is having your own bedroom. And hot water. And heating. And all my friends at school.'

However, mum Helen is as determined as any other traveller mum that her children grow up steeped in their cultural identity and traditions. Each summer, she takes them out in a trailer to mingle with their cousins, who still live on a site. 'I don't want them to lose that. I want them to remain part of the community.'

And in another way, Helen is following traveller tradition to the letter. Katie and brother John are taking their Communion vows with the rest of their school year, who are all settled kids. Most parents want their kids to fit in, but not Helen. Katie will dazzle in a Nico Communion frock.

'You really do want to be the pick of the bunch,' says Helen. 'And settled children, English children as we call them, don't really have the style of the travellers, so they only go for little simple and plain dresses with not much detail. So I hope that day that she turns heads.'

Helen realises that neither Katie nor her brother truly understand the religious significance of the day. 'Well, because they are children, they don't really know the importance of it,' she says. 'To them, it is just this big dress. The girls are done up like a little bride. They are a million dollars and they think that this day is theirs, which it is. But religion-wise, they haven't really got the full clue about it.'

As Katie emerges in her large, white, shimmering frock,

she looks thrilled. 'I think that I look like a blonde Pocahontas. Like a princess. It is nice, gorgeous,' she says.

Helen responds, 'You're beautiful, like a mini-bride.' It seems weddings are never far from the mind of a traveller mum.

Thelma asks Katie if she picked the dress out herself on a recent trip to Nico. 'My mum came the first time and she picked it.'

Once again, it seems as though it's mum living out the fairy-tale fantasy.

'I look like a mini-bride, and I like the crown because it's so sparkly and diamondy. I likes Swarovski.'

Four Communions and a Christening, starring Paddy Doherty, set in East Croydon, South London. Paddy is about to become godfather to Angela, newborn daughter of his cousin Tony. Paddy is outside the church, holding Angela in his arms, showing her off. Seems it's OK for a traveller man to hold a baby, after all.

'This is baby Angela! She's getting christened. A little beauty queen, God bless her. Look at this – they've got the toenails painted! Is that a little picture or what is it? You could just put her in your mouth and swallow her.'

Paddy has driven all the way down from Manchester – some 200 miles – to 'stand' for little Angela. Turns out he's a serial godfather.

'I am the godfather I say, no exaggeration, to the best part of about eighty-two children. With every child I really am on it. You give it your heart and soul. If you don't give your heart and soul, then don't do it, because you are a hypocrite.'

He explains what it means to be asked. 'It's an honour. It's more than an honour. It's a privilege! They're treating you with a lot of respect. When you ask someone to do this, it means you have the utmost respect for that person. It's a big thing. It's not just any divvy you'll ask. You'd ask no village idiot boy, would you? You're gonna ask a person who, if anything happens, is gonna take care of your family and mind them and mind your child.'

Paddy tells us what happens at a typical christening, post-church. 'It's just party time then. Have a few pints, more than likely someone will have a slap as well at the same time! I hope not, but it happens. What the fuck can you do? Travellers is travellers, aren't they, and young fellas is young fellas.'

Later, we catch up with three of the four kids who've taken their Communion vows today. How they describe their outfits tells its own story.

Angela, eight, goes first. 'My dress is nice because it's got loads of diamonds. I look like a mini-bride, and I like the crown because it's so sparkly and diamondy. I likes Swarovski. My mum did my make-up. She does my make-up all the time, like when I go to parties and stuff. She always puts glitter on me and a bit of lipstick, but I don't like being too done up. I'm only a child.'

Her friend Lizzie talks about her equally dazzling

creation. 'My dress has got loads of these sequins and little diamonds and roses on it. I'm wearing a necklace and the earrings, but that's all the jewellery I've got on because I don't want to look overdressed and fake. I'm only a child. The diamond earrings are a bit heavy and they do hurt me ears a bit, but you have to go through pain, like me mummy says. No pain no gain. Pain for beauty.'

Finally, Bernadette, seven, knows the look she prefers. 'I like to look like Katie Price. My dress has got feathers and diamonds, and it's black on the inside.'

Several hours later, the godfather is a little unsteady on his feet. Thankfully, he's no longer holding baby Angela.

'It has been fantastic,' says Paddy. 'There are no domestics. No nothing. A couple of young fellas shouting and that was it. It is just lovely to see my brother and to see his wife and my nieces and nephews. They all come over and hug you and kiss you like you are really important. You might not think that you are important, but to them, you are important. It is beautiful.'

Paddy and his wife, Roseanne, are devout Catholics. He explains why Angela's christening today galvanises the sense of a thriving and enduring traveller community. 'She's bred to be a Christian! She'll do her Holy Communion and make her confirmation, please God! She'll get married and have children, and her children will do the same and bring their children up the same. It's how we've been reared up.

'After weddings, christenings and Holy Communions are the biggest thing in the whole world, aren't they? You're doing the best for your child. You've done what is your duty.'

There's also the social aspect. Paddy's from Manchester. Travellers have made it here from Scotland and Wales and from all over England.

'That's nice, isn't it? It shows you Tony's well respected. And there's young men and girls who'll meet here today and they'll get together and they will marry and bring their kids up the same. It's the traveller lifecycle.'

Postscript

Josie and Swanley Smith are currently living in Uxbridge along with their newborn daughter, also named Josie. 'You know it is love when you love your baby as much as you love sunbeds and Red Bull!' they point out.

Lizzie Lee and the three Bridgets – Ward, Rooney and Doran – have all had babies.

Sam Norton and Pat Skye Lee are expecting their first child in November 2011.

Noreen McDonagh is leaving ABC Cakes to go and work full time in a local hair salon.

Thelma Madine's dressmaking business is booming. She has orders for the next two years and has received enquiries from the USA and Australia.

The residents of Dale Farm in Essex have been issued with a 28 days' notice to quit.

Cheyenne Pidgley, now sixteen, has been 'asked for' by Jon McFadden, the boy who grabbed her at Josie and Swanley's wedding. Cheyenne's parents have agreed to the marriage on the proviso that her sixteen-year-old suitor first passes his driving test so that he can earn a living.